Brilliant Customer Success

Managing the Customer Experience for Profitable Growth and Brand Dominance

Praise for *Brilliant Customer Success*

"James Alexander does it again! Following previous books relevant to enhancing customer experiences, his latest edition, *Brilliant Customer Success*, captures the essence of practical applications for organizations to implement in their day-to-day activities. A must-read for anyone in a leadership position."

Brian D. Osswald
Vice President, Sales and Service USA
Acute Care Therapies
Getinge

"Crisp, concise, and complete. A must-read for those who are serious about the customer success journey."

Joseph W. Wood
Global Vice President, Commercial Vehicles
Axalta Coating Systems

"This book is just like its author—bold and direct in its statements of what can and what can't work. Clear and easy to read, the book is just the right mix of practical theory and real-life experience."

Mary Trick
Chief Customer Officer
Infor

"If you're interested in better managing both your customer's destiny along with your company's, then read this book. Alex has written a comprehensive yet to-the-point guide to managing your customer experience. He provides much to ponder about your customer's needs, your people, and your organization, BUT most importantly, he delivers the actions to take to make an immediate positive impact!"

Graham Irwin
President and CEO
Irwin Seating Company

"Valuable and practical, straightforward and clear, a pleasure to read."

Terry Jansen
President and Founder
PSVillage

"*Brilliant Customer Success* is, in nutshell, a brilliant piece of work! Alex has taken the complex topic of customer success and provided a clear foundational road map for delivering profitable customer success in any size organization."

Aaron Woods
Director, ASP Relationship and Programs,
Lean Six Sigma Certified Green Belt
Xerox US Channels Group/Channel Partner Operations

"*Brilliant Customer Success* is engaging and insightful. Alex will change your mind about the way you acquire, grow, and maintain customers. This is the new primer for customer success."

Steve Lieberson
Senior Vice President, Sales
Guardian TOS

"*Brilliant Customer Success* provides great insight into what real customer success is all about. Every company pretends to care about making their customers successful, but very few are able to deliver on this promise. Alex provides his wisdom, backed up by solid research, and provides a simple road map for how to seriously implement a customer success program within your company."

John Hamilton
President
Service Strategies Corporation

"Customer success is highly cited, but is not wholly understood as a mindset, a leadership path, and an operational guide to growth. This engaging book guides you to that critical path for success!"

Jeanne Bliss
Cofounder
Customer Experience Professionals Association and
Author, Chief Customer Officer 2.0

"This book provides concrete strategies for delivering brilliant customer success. Alex has a superb track record for working with companies to transform technical resources into revenue producers. For companies that are seeking workforce transformation, this book is a must-read."

Mark Fair
Vice President, Cloud Services
Epicor Software

"Alex does it again! From the Hassle Meter to the Personal Change Meter, this book contains just the right mix of theory, best practices, and real-world advice. I highly recommend it."

Thomas Schlick
Vice President
Sterilmed Inc., a part of the Johnson & Johnson Family of Companies

"Alexander's new book, *Brilliant Customer Success*, is, in a word, brilliant. It is short and easy to read, but don't let that fool you. It is a very powerful little book. Alex makes the important point that if you are a cloud company or a SaaS company, or getting into any subscription-based business, you need to take customer success seriously. It covers both customer experience and customer success in a very concise way. Alex writes with undisguised humor in easy-to-digest chunks. If you are on the journey to customer success, this book provides the road map and offers many graphs, tools, checklists, and guides to get you there. A very valuable book if you are interested in customer success."

Al Hahn
Executive Director
The Association of Support Professionals

"Alex shows, with simple precision, how to establish trust and delight your customers with a success approach that is fun to read and exciting to go execute."

Peter Szary
Global Vice President, Consulting Services
Qlik

Brilliant Customer Success

Managing the Customer Experience for Profitable Growth and Brand Dominance

James "Alex" Alexander

Alexander Consulting

Brilliant Customer Success:
Managing the Customer Experience for Profitable Growth and
Brand Dominance

© 2016 James A. Alexander

This edition published by Alexander Consulting, Fort Myers, FL.

All rights reserved. Published in the United States of America.
No part of this book may be used or reproduced in any manner
whatsoever without the written permission of Alexander Consulting.

First Edition

ISBN 978-0-9832260-3-1

Table of Contents

Introduction: Brilliant Customer Success	1
The Marvelous Opportunity	1
Today's Customer Success Reality	2
Why This Book?	3
Book Objectives	4
Who Will Benefit from This Book	5
Book Background	6
First Some Definitions	7
A Final Word to the Reader	12
Overview: The Brilliant Customer Success Performance Chain	15
Business Results	16
Customer Impact	16
Touchpoint Management	20
Overview Summary	22
Chapter 1: The Transition from Customer "Happy Talk" to Customer Success	23
A Quick Look Back in Time	23
Customer-Centric Organizations Outperform Everyone Else	24
Customer-First Litmus Test for a Traditional Organization	24
Most Important Customer Success Challenges	27
Chapter Summary	32

Chapter 2: Brilliant Customer Experiences	33
Brilliant Customer Experiences: The Seven Things Your Customers Want, Expect, and Deserve	34
What Does the Customer Get?	36
Implications of Poor Customer Experience	37
Customer Experience Realities	38
The Two Contributors to Brilliant Customer Experiences	39
Making Chicken Soup Out of Chicken Feathers	46
Develop a Brilliant Service Recovery Approach	46
Create a Brilliant Service Recovery Process	47
Excite and Empower Your Team	50
But What If It's Not Our Fault?	50
Chapter Summary	51
Chapter 3: Brilliant Employees	53
From Traditional Frontline Personnel to Brilliant Customer Success Team	54
Comparison: Cloud versus Everyone Else	59
Findings from the Study	59
Recommendations	61
Chapter Summary	61
Chapter 4: Brilliant Performance Systems	63
Structured Functions to Fluid Processes	65
Customer Success Approach	65
Customer Success Marketing Performance System	68
Customer Success Selling Performance System	70
Enabling Technology	74
Chapter Summary	75

Chapter 5: Touchpoint Management — 77
- Cruising Vacation Example — 79
- Step One: Aligning Supplier Focus to Help the Customer Clarify Issues — 79
- Step Two: Aligning Supplier Promoting to Help the Customer Define Requirements — 83
- Step Three: Aligning Supplier Qualifying to Help the Customer Consider Choices — 85
- Step Four: Committing the Customer to Make a Decision — 91
- Step Five: Delivering on the Promise to Help the Customer Evaluate Results — 94
- Step Six: Growing the Account to Help Renew and Expand — 99
- Touchpoint Management Study Findings — 101
- Touchpoint Management Recommendations — 102
- Chapter Summary — 104

Chapter 6: Brilliant Leadership — 105
- Culture — 105
- Culture of Success — 107
- Compelling Blueprint — 107
- Study Findings Related to Leadership — 108
- Leadership Recommendations — 109
- Leading Brilliant Change — 111
- Rationality: Does It Make Sense? — 113
- Commitment: Will Management Follow Through? — 113
- Fairness: Is It Fair to the Customer, My Peers, and Me? — 114
- Value: How Good a Deal Is It for Me? — 114
- Chapter Summary — 115

References and Notes — 117

INTRODUCTION

Brilliant Customer Success

The Marvelous Opportunity

Customer success. The phrase has a nice ring to it. It rolls off the tongue smoothly, like "boundless beauty," or "endless summer," or "green chili cheeseburgers." It sounds almost patriotic! Who could be against customer success?

But just what is it? What's in it for your organization? What's in it for you? Should you stay seated on your lounge chair, dip your toes in the water, or take the dive off the high board?

You are not alone in facing this dilemma, this challenge, this marvelous opportunity. Lots of smart people in organizations all over the planet are pondering, defining, and testing customer success in an effort to figure it out.

The potential exists for you to drive buckets full of profitable growth and totally dominate your competitors…to be the go-to supplier in your marketplace…to have prospects standing in line to work with you! However, let's ground our thinking with the customer success reality.

Today's Customer Success Reality

Research and experience show the reality of the customer success journey in today's organizations:
- **Young ballerinas and old firefighters.** There is a hodgepodge in both the maturity levels of customer success initiatives within organizations and the approaches they are taking to make it a reality—some use finesse, while others try brute force. Some are bold, but many are hesitant, having one foot on the boat and one foot on the dock. Organizations clearly have different definitions, goals, issues, processes, and metrics related to customer success.
- **Lots of moving parts.** Like a NASA rocket launch, many variables impact the mission. Customer success impacts all functions and most all personnel in the organization; its implementation requires a holistic approach.
- **From Manchester to Mumbai.** For some traditional businesses, customer success is an alien landscape, thus, this transition requires rethinking old truths and reexamining ways of doing business. Implementing customer success requires all the attention of major organization change, and leading this transformation will sometimes require Kevlar vests and iron underwear.
- **Skipping piano practice.** Many organizations attempting a customer success model are unprepared for the change (especially as it relates to culture) and, hence, face an out-of-tune failure. Issuing press releases announcing your commitment to customer success, but only changing the titles on the business cards of your sales and services people to "customer success manager," or appointing Fred as the new "customer success champion," but giving him no funding (i.e., not do-

ing the heavy lifting required) ain't going to get you a gig at Harry's Bar, let alone at Carnegie Hall.
- **Genome mapping.** New technologies offer amazing capabilities that can impact customer success, but a high percentage of organizations have issues concerning the quality of the information they have, compared to what they feel they need. Compasses and sextants still have their place, but satellite phones, GPSs, and night vision optics are so much better.
- **Critical mass.** Many organizations question whether they have the correct talent to deliver customer success effectively and consistently. Yet, few make any changes to their recruiting, hiring, training, or coaching practices. Pack mules are great for long-haul loads, but quarter horses and Arabians are much better for quick maneuvering.
- **Improv and ad lib.** In many organizations, there are role and responsibility disconnects that add waste to the system and cause confusion for the customer. A common practice with big suppliers is to bolt a customer success group on top of whatever structure is already in place. They hope for improved performance, but the result is just actors on stage unsure of their lines.
- **Warp drive: a need for speed.** Very active involvement of customer-facing personnel in the first days directly after purchase (the magical month) is now a requirement, not a nice-to-do. For traditional businesses used to having several months (or even years) to show impact, this is like taking a golf cart on the Autobahn.

Why This Book?

Even with all the challenges, building customer success is worth the effort. Whether a traditional product company selling on-premise offerings or an off-premise organization selling outsourced solutions or cloud-based subscriptions, suppliers that deliver customer success reap both higher profits and deeper loyalty than organizations that don't.[1] Hence, having a clear understanding of what customer success is and how to deliver it has immense potential value to most all organizations.

In addition, for organizations in complex, competitive environments, building customer success may not be an option, but a requirement...a mandate for survival, demanding some behaviors and philosophies quite different from traditional ways of doing business. Yet, as my research confirms, customer success is defined and implemented in many different ways—core practices are just being defined, processes are in their infancy, and different business models are being tested.

These are interesting times in the business world!

Book Objectives

- Define customer success and related terms in meaningful, actionable ways.
- Provide a robust customer success model flexible enough to apply in most organizations (little or huge, B2B or B2C, on-premise or off-premise, business or non-profit).
- Outline the requirements and the core, best, and brilliant practices for delivering customer success.
- Predict the potholes on the path to performance and point out how to prevent (or at least mediate) them.
- Elaborate the changes organization leaders must implement to move from customer success "happy talk" to purposeful action.
- Explain the important customer success similarities and differences between the traditional on-site license model and the recurring revenue model.
- Identify the important issues, metrics, and expectations of customer success at all organization levels.
- Understand the necessary knowledge, skills, and mindsets

required of the personnel tasked with delivering customer success, whatever their title.
- Determine the key actions that will speed and smooth the customer success journey.
- Provide you with ideas on how to lead the customer success transition, demonstrate your brilliance, keep your sanity, and have fun doing it.

Who Will Benefit from This Book?

There is direct application of the contents of this book to anyone interested in delivering customer success and receiving the profitable growth and brand dominance that result. Although much of the verbiage within this book is business-oriented, the basic concepts and content are viable for any type of organization wishing to gain from becoming customer laser-focused.

Executives will find value in learning:
- A clear and applicable definition of customer success and related terms.
- Ways to calculate the economic benefits of adopting a customer success model.
- A performance chain that provides a robust model of customer success applicable to most all businesses.
- Why your customers' experiences with your organization are much poorer than you think…and are costing you lots of money.
- The major differences between traditional and cloud-based delivery of customer success.
- Why your current culture may need to evolve if you embrace a customer-centric organizational philosophy.
- The requirements in leading the transition to a customer success model.

Marketing, sales, services, and support leaders will discover:

- A customer success framework for enhancing customer success.
- Peer learning to compare and contrast against their current customer success activities.
- Key benchmarks and core practices.
- Recommendations that can be applied for immediate performance improvement.

Frontline professionals will learn:
- A clearer understanding of the "big picture," and their vital role in making customer success a reality.
- The importance of expanding their capabilities and assuming new roles.
- The factors most important to their ongoing success.

Researchers, academics, practitioners, or anyone tasked with improving the performance of organizations will benefit from having available:
- An actionable customer success model.
- Worst practices and how to avoid them.
- Guidelines to successfully implement customer success.

Book Background

This book is based upon the growing body of customer success literature and the author's and his colleagues' experience in consulting, coaching, and training organizations on how to build and grow customer success capabilities.

Furthermore, throughout the book I will share findings from my customer success research involving 94 companies from the technology industry.[2] The individuals interviewed (managers and executives from mainly medium to large firms) are either leading their organizations' customer success initiatives or are members of their companies' customer success teams.

First Some Definitions

"Customer success" is a term bantered about in boardrooms and breakrooms in many different ways. It has been perceived as a business model, a company-wide priority, an organization, a profession, or a technology.[3] My research confirmed this disparity — the definitions given regarding customer success and customer success management were as varied as Mexican chilies at Santa Fe's Saturday farmers' market.

> **Dim Practice:** Sadly, several participants admitted (sometimes sheepishly) that there was no customer success definition at all in their organization.
>
> **Flash Point:** If you don't know where you are going, any path will do, but you might end up bruised, battered, and bleeding in a ditch. Take the time to clearly define what customer success means in your organization and communicate it again and again. Below is my thinking to get you started.

In this book I will try to influence you to embrace customer success as a strategy and philosophy that becomes embedded in your culture. I will share with you a customer success performance model that I hope you will adopt. But an important understanding is that customer success is personal. Just as kids in a candy store might prefer different treats, each customer may value certain outcomes more highly than others at a given point in time, and hence, customer success varies from person-to-person. So I prefer a concrete, actionable definition.

Customer Success
I define customer success as a customer state of mind, in which a specific customer (let's call her a key player) feels that she has achieved her desires (business outcomes and personal wins)

while undergoing brilliant customer experiences. Here are the three requirements of customer success:

- **Business outcomes.** The results that a key player hopes will happen to her organization from purchasing and using a supplier's offerings (e.g., increased revenue, lowered downtime, enhanced productivity).
- **Personal wins.** The results that a key player hopes will happen directly to her from purchasing and/or using a supplier's offerings (e.g., job security, personal recognition, less job hassle).
- **Customer experience.** The customer's perception of a supplier's performance, including activities that do not directly touch the customer but that affect the customer's overall view of the supplier. Brilliant customer experience occurs when the seven things that customers want, expect, and deserve are met (details in Chapter 2).

Customer Success Brilliant Performance Chain
The overall model of customer success management linking all aspects of supplier performance that effectively deliver customer success to key players and yield the supplier's desired results is illustrated in the Customer Success Brilliant Performance Chain.

Customer Decision-Making Process
This process consists of the six defined steps (clarifying issues, defining requirements, considering choices, making decisions, evaluating results, renewing and expanding) that every customer goes through when making important decisions.

Touchpoint Management
Touchpoint management is the alignment of the six defined steps (focusing, promoting, qualifying, committing, delivering, and growing) that every customer-focused supplier goes through to properly synch with the customer's decision-making process,

providing appropriate, credible, relevant, usable information, while delivering brilliant customer experiences at every customer touchpoint.

Customer Success Team
The customer success team comprises all supplier personnel that, as a team, are tasked with delivering relevant information and brilliant customer experiences that lead to customer success. Note that everyone in your organization should have the responsibility to contribute to customer success. However, for the purpose of this book, the customer success team will be considered those responsible for marketing, selling, and servicing/supporting.

Traditional Organization
In the traditional model, the supplier sells offerings (e.g., hardware, software licenses) that are housed at the customer's location. In many cases, the customer makes a large initial investment and often has internal people assigned to supporting the supplier offering. Depending upon the complexity of the offering sold, the traditional organization may sell other services, such as service contracts, professional services, or consulting.

Subscription Organization
Often referred to as a cloud-based, software-as-a-service (SaaS), or recurring revenue business, the customers of a subscription organization do not buy the offering of the supplier. They instead pay a monthly, quarterly, or annual fee dependent upon usage of the supplier offering. The customer does not own the supplier offering—they lease its usage for an agreed length of time.

Example: Other Differences Between a Traditional Business and a Subscription Business
Let me take things one step forward by providing an example

comparing a supplier selling enterprise software. Let's start with the customer perspective, seen on the next page.

Customer Perspective	Traditional	Subscription
External Supplier Investment	Large to Huge	Small
Internal Investment to Support	Lots	Almost None
Perceived Importance	Very High	Medium
Perceived Risk	High to Very High	Low to Medium
Decision Makers	Senior Management	Varies
Expected Time to Value	Months, Sometimes Years	First Week
Switching Costs	Almost Unbearable	Not Much

Enterprise software involves and impacts all parts of a business. For many customers, their initial investment in buying the software licenses from a traditional supplier can be millions of dollars. Also the customer will pay the supplier big bucks over the years for expert support and software upgrades. Internal investment can be quite large, as well, and could include new hardware (servers, routers, and so on) necessary for the software, a large staff of talented people to administer the software, and management required to supervise this talent.

If the software is accessible via subscription, the external investment is several zeros shorter than purchasing it—instead of spending millions, it could be just tens of thousands of dollars per month with a one-year commitment. The internal investment needed to support the software would probably be miniscule, as all the costs of support are the responsibility of the supplier.

Because the purchase from a traditional supplier is so big and highly visible, it is seen as a very important investment to the customer. Furthermore, big investments mean high perceived risk, especially for the executive who recommends and implements the solution. On the other hand, since the investment is significantly lower in the subscription agreement, the perceived risk is seen as much lower. Often decisions will be made further down the chain of command.

Most buyers of complex products like enterprise software have learned the hard way that it can easily take a year (or two or three) to have things up and running and performing at least close to expectations. However, those leasing enterprise software from a subscription provider expect results immediately. Hence, time to value (time required to get the promised results) is thought of in weeks.

Considering the abandonment of a big-ticket, complex, slow-return (or no-return) investment makes even the most stoic executive sweat like a Swede in the Sahara. Every effort will be given to a nonperforming supplier to change his ways. Yes, switching costs exist in the subscription model, but compared to traditional models, it is like comparing a ripple in a kiddie wading pool to a tsunami.

Now for the supplier perspective, shown below.

Supplier Perspective	Traditional	Subscription
Philosophy	Sell the Big Deal at Any Cost	Customer First
Distinct Competencies	Big-Deal Selling	On-Boarding
Key Financial Metric	Gross Revenue	ARR or MRR
Adoption	Nice	Critical
Retention	Good to Have	Critical
Emotional Loyalty	Important	Vital
Customer Success	Nice Slogan!	Strategy and Philosophy

In the world of the traditional software company, sales is the top dog, and building sales capabilities is the most important competency (yes, more important than product development, quality control, and support). The sales focus is to get the big deal…whatever it takes. The reason is that most of the money the supplier will acquire from this customer occurs at this one point in time. Gross revenue from new customers is the key financial metric, with win-rate the tactical indicator.

In the world of subscriptions, the philosophy is customer-centric. The subscription company knows that it won't even breakeven on a new account for a year or more, hence, all things must be customer dipped. All aspects of dealing with the customer are important, but the vital competence is on-boarding — getting the customer comfortably, confidently, capably, and quickly using the software.

Subscription companies would, of course, like to get lots of new business, however, they know that churn rate is their demon to control. Hence, recurring revenue, measured monthly and/or annually, is the number they watch most.

To the traditional supplier, "customer success" makes a great marketing slogan, and for many that is about it. For the subscription company it is the strategy and mindset that aligns with the customer-first philosophy. Delivering customer success is the business.

> *The biggest concern? The key you must learn?*
> *On-board with speed, meet every need,*
> *And you'll have no issue with churn.*

For another comparison, check out *Customer Success*.[4] The book is an excellent resource for any organization interested in this topic.

A Final Word to the Reader

This book addresses an important topic that deserves serious attention. In fact, I've devoted many years of my life to learning the ins and outs of organization performance and the key contributors to success. However, I've attempted to add a dash of humor and the occasional tongue-in-cheek comment to make the writing process more fun for me and the reading process more enjoyable for you. Your tolerance is appreciated if my mixed metaphors or attempts at jocularity miss their intended mark!

OVERVIEW

The Brilliant Customer Success Performance Chain

In this overview I introduce the Brilliant Customer Success Performance Chain, shown in Figure 1. It is a robust model applicable to most all organizations for planning, building, implementing, monitoring, diagnosing, and enhancing customer success results.

Figure 1 The Brilliant Customer Success Performance Chain

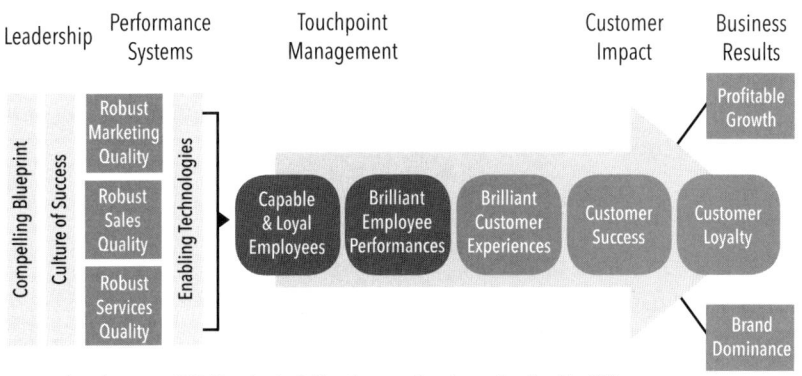

Leadership | Performance Systems | Touchpoint Management | Customer Impact | Business Results

- Compelling Blueprint
- Culture of Success
- Robust Marketing Quality
- Robust Sales Quality
- Robust Services Quality
- Enabling Technologies
- Capable & Loyal Employees
- Brilliant Employee Performances
- Brilliant Customer Experiences
- Customer Success
- Customer Loyalty
- Profitable Growth
- Brand Dominance

Source: Alexander, James. 2015. "Creating the Brilliant Customer Experience – Part One: The Brilliant Performance Chain."

I will start our discussion on the far right side of the chain and work backward. Following chapters will discuss each chain link in appropriate detail.

Business Results

Business results are your reward for doing customer success right. Selfishly, your desired outcome as the supplier is business results. Yes, there can be a multitude of preferable outcomes, but for most organizations there are two vital business results that trump all others—new streams of profitable growth to fund the future of the business, plus brand dominance based upon a reputation superior to your rivals.

Flash Point: Let the potential gain smooth the probable pain. For readers that sign on for the customer success journey, there will be potholes on the path to performance as there always are when doing something important. Taking time up front to realistically calculate the value you will receive from making brilliant customer success a reality will harden your resolve when times get challenging. Start with calculating the lifetime value of your best prospects/customers. Quantify what the financial return will be when you are the "go to" supplier in your space. Consider the positive impact of increased win-rates and improved retention. Keeping this in mind will soothe your soul when the roof leaks, the pipes break, and cracks occur in the foundation.

Customer Impact

Customer loyalty drives business results. Loads of research over the last several years show that the loyalty of your customers is a prime driver of the business results discussed above. There is a direct relationship. Loyal customers buy more and more, again and again, rarely quibbling over price.[1] Emotionally, loyal customers tout your attributes far and wide and gladly provide testimonials to woo your prospects for you. Loyal customers are the crown jewels of your resources and should be guarded as a miser would a strongbox. If we embrace the eminent management consultant Peter Drucker's declaration that the purpose of a business is to get and grow customers, customer loyalty is the secret sauce of the recipe (Figure 2).[2]

Figure 2 Customer Impact Drives Supplier Business Results

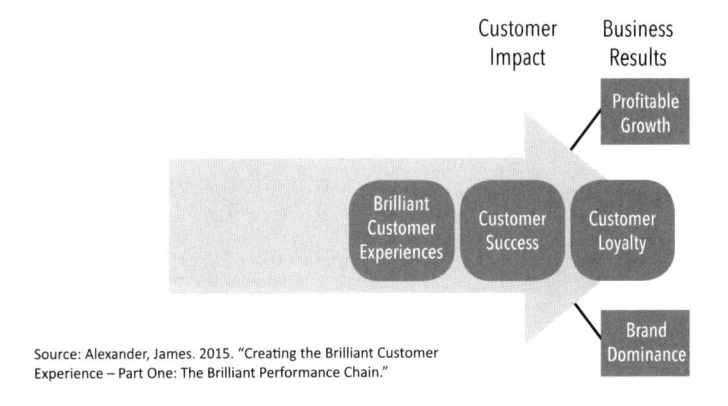

Source: Alexander, James. 2015. "Creating the Brilliant Customer Experience – Part One: The Brilliant Performance Chain."

Customer success drives customer loyalty. To earn that loyalty, you must deliver customer success as each key player in the customer account defines it. This may sound daunting, because you have lots of key players in your base of business.

Flash Point: Categorize to prioritize. It is nice to proclaim that you are dedicated to delivering customer success to all customers. However, if your resources are limited (aren't they always?), the reality is you can't do it today, and you probably won't be able to do it tomorrow. Maybe eventually, but not in the near to mid-future.

So my recommendation is that you categorize your customers so that you can prioritize your efforts.

Figure 3 shows the three customer importance categories, your desired customer outcomes for each category, plus my recommended approach to each category.

Figure 3 Segmenting Customers by Importance

Importance Category	Nice-to-Have	Want-to-Have	Must-Have
Desired Customer Outcome	Tolerance	Acceptance	Success
Supplier Approach	Standard	Tailored	Custom

Must-Have Customers
Your must-have customers are the ones that will take you into the future. These are your strategic accounts, those with the highest lifetime value potential. Seek their loyalty first. Your goal is to help them achieve customer success as they define it, and you will dedicate any and all resources needed. Your one-to-one approach means that you will customize your offering and do what it takes to make these vital customers extremely pleased to have you as a supplier.

Want-to-Have Customers
Your second most important customer category is your want-to-have customers. Yes, you'd love to help them achieve success, but because of resource limitations you hope that you can just keep them satisfied. Your one-to-many approach allows you to try to tailor your offerings to their uniqueness. However, you realize that customers in this category will change suppliers if they perceive a better deal, as satisfied customers are not loyal customers.

Nice-to-Have Customers
Finally, there are your nice-to-have customers. Once again, be-

cause of your limited resources, you cannot customize or even tailor your offering for them. The standard offering you provide often means that they are not particularly happy with you but they keep you as a supplier because they don't want the hassle of switching, or it is just not worth the effort to get another supplier. Your desired outcome is that they will tolerate your lack of attention enough to keep you as a supplier.

Not sure where to classify your accounts? Figure 4 reveals a simple but powerful tool that looks at six dynamics of importance. Use this as is, or season it to your taste — just develop a standard tool that everyone understands and everyone uses.

Figure 4 Account Criteria Screen

Potential Account _____	Rating
	Strongly Disgree Strongly Agree 1 2 3 4 5
1. **Importance**: They see our type of offerings and capabilities as critical to their success.	
2. **Attitude**: They value a business partner relationship.	
3. **Credibility**: They possess a strong brand in the marketplace.	
4. **Potential**: We have the possibility of big, long-term business growth.	
5. **Innovation**: We can learn from them.	
6. **Cultural Fit**: Our organizations share common norms and ways of thinking.	
TOTAL	

Flash Point: When it comes to scaling success, if you are in the early stages of customer success, the one-to-one approach outlined for must-have customers is my recommended starting point. Your learnings there will help you streamline and hopefully automate some important tasks. Additionally, applying the findings from your industry/market/geography segmentation research will show you that key players with similar roles will have similar desired business outcomes and personal wins. This will help make your one-to-some approach in tailoring your offerings a higher-probability fit with the customers in this category. It also will improve the appeal of your standard offering for your nice-to-have customers and make your one-to-many approach more efficient.

Also, as your customer success experience grows, your enhanced technology, system sophistication, and improved process management, especially touchpoint management, will help customers' perceptions improve within all three classifications.

Brilliant customer experiences enable customer success. The promise of customer success requires brilliant customer experiences. Like the catalyst in a chemical reaction, a brilliant customer experience releases the full potential of a supplier-customer relationship. Customer experience is shaped at every touchpoint — every encounter or contact the customer has with your organization. How to deliver brilliant customer experiences is discussed very soon in Chapter 2 and throughout the remainder of the book.

Touchpoint Management

Brilliant employee performances drive brilliant customer experiences (Figure 5). The more closely your people give the customer what they need, want, and expect at each step in their decision-making process, the more powerful the moment of truth, and the more likely the customer will invite you to participate in their next decision step.

Capable and loyal employees are required to deliver brilliant employee performances. Your frontline personnel must have the capabilities needed to interact with the customer the right way at the right time.

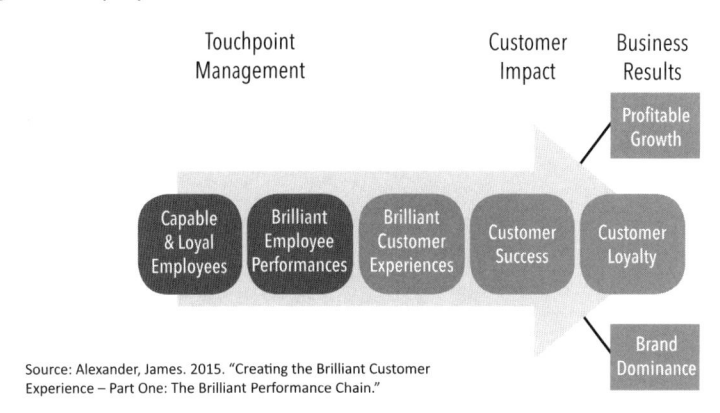

Figure 5 Employee Performance Drives Customer Success

Touchpoint Management | Customer Impact | Business Results

Capable & Loyal Employees → Brilliant Employee Performances → Brilliant Customer Experiences → Customer Success → Customer Loyalty → Profitable Growth / Brand Dominance

Source: Alexander, James. 2015. "Creating the Brilliant Customer Experience – Part One: The Brilliant Performance Chain."

Chapter 3 will outline the five required capabilities of the customer success team that are constantly deployed, but with varying intensity based upon the situation. This chapter will also explain the transition that many frontline people will need to make from the tactical, reactive requirements of their old job to the proactive, strategic, relationship-based needs of delivering brilliant customer success. It will bring out the importance of quality training and consistent reinforcement to make the change stick.

Performance systems provide the information and tools required to help your capable and loyal employees in their moments of truth (Figure 6). Chapter 4 outlines what is needed, focusing on marketing, selling, and servicing. Chapter 5 puts it all together in aligning the six supplier business development steps to the six customer decision-making steps.

Leadership drives the bus in creating a culture of success and building and implementing a compelling blueprint to guide implementation (Figure 7). As we all know, if the big dogs don't get off the porch, the pack doesn't hunt. I will recommend specific actions for leaders that will to turn the crank on the customer success machine. Chapter 6 covers what is needed and how to pull it off.

Figure 6 Performance Systems Enable Employee Performance

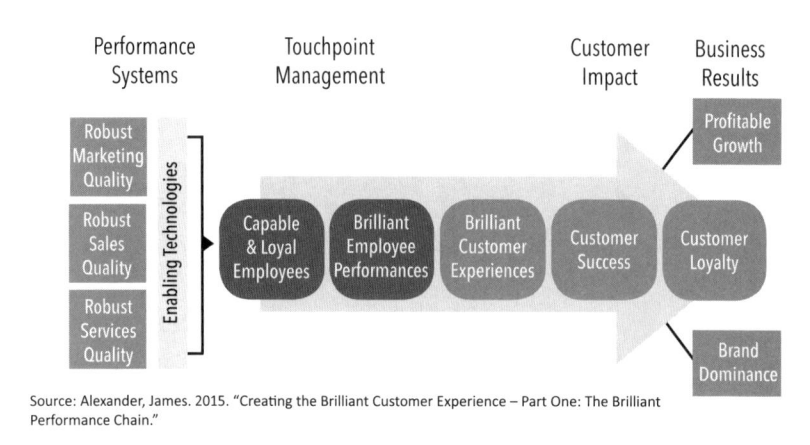

Source: Alexander, James. 2015. "Creating the Brilliant Customer Experience – Part One: The Brilliant Performance Chain."

Figure 7 Leadership Creates a Culture of Success

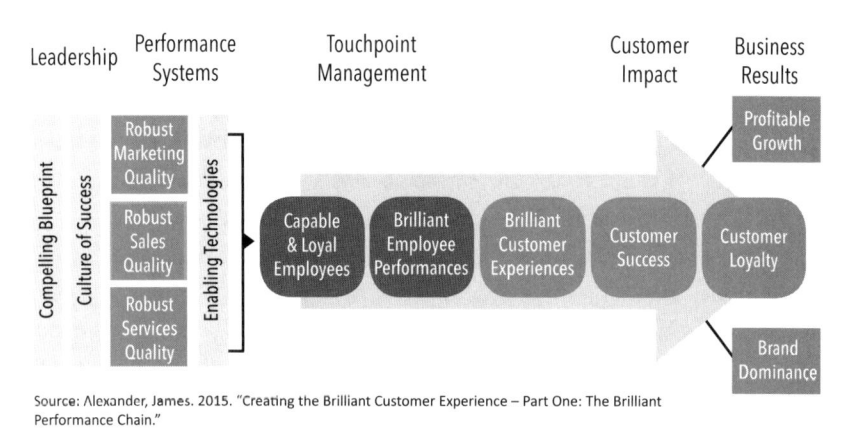

Source: Alexander, James. 2015. "Creating the Brilliant Customer Experience – Part One: The Brilliant Performance Chain."

Overview Summary

By now you have broken the code…each link in the performance chain is dependent on the link to its immediate left. For the chain to be effective, each link must be strong.

Next, we deepen our understanding of this performance chain starting with discussing brilliant customer experiences.

CHAPTER 1

The Transition from Customer "Happy Talk" to Customer Success

A Quick Look Back in Time

Distinguished readers (those with the gray hairs of experience) will recall a bookcase full of volumes going back decades touting the importance of the customer. Business authors bandied about bushel baskets full of phrases such as "the customer is #1," "customer delight," "uncommon service," "knock-your-socks-off service," and on and on.

The intent was clear: Embrace the customer and all ailments will be healed…the blind will see and the lame will walk.

This wave of customer inspiration led to mission, vision, and value statements being drawn up (mainly by the marketing folks) and hung in lobbies and posted in company dining rooms all over the planet proclaiming, pledging, and promising the organization's commitment to the customer.

Customer-Centric Organizations Outperform Everyone Else

Sophisticated readers (add wrinkles to the gray hairs) will also recall that study after study has demonstrated the positive financial impact of acting on this customer philosophy, whether called a "customer-centric organization" or a "culture embracing customer intimacy" or something similar.[1]

Hard numbers provided positive proof that true customer focus made absolute business sense. No doubt about it, any organization serious about outstanding performance had to grab and hold tight to the ring of customer focus.

So logically, after 30-plus years, this customer philosophy should be the norm, the standard operating procedure, the driving concept embedded in the business strategy and enacted in the business plan of the majority of both profit and nonprofit entities.

But is customer-centricity a prime driver of today's organizations? How about your company? Let's take a test and find out.

Customer-First Litmus Test for a Traditional Organization

Think about your organization for a minute. I bet you have at least one customer-hugging slogan hanging in your lobby. Here is the situation: It is the last day of the last quarter of your fiscal year, and it is crunch time. Your place is a-flutter with activity like an F5 tornado in a Kansas trailer park…sales guys with sweat on their brows and phones in both ears are doing the Selling Two-Step.

Cold reality sets in around the executive boardroom as the truth is told that the only way for your organization to make the revenue numbers (and thus qualify the executives to get their bonuses) is to ship product that is not quite ready for prime time (known bugs in the software or hardware missing a vital part that for all practical purposes makes your offering inoperable). The CFO solemnly states that the rules of business finance allow that shipping this product will count immediately as recognized revenue whether the product is functional or not. It is up to the executive team to decide. So, does your company ship the sub-quality product knowing it will be worse than doing nothing for the customer?

Well, your organization may be different, but most organizations in that situation will ship the product. The numbers are made, the bonuses paid, and the customer commitment betrayed. Leave it to the services guys to apologize, agonize, and minimize the damage of lost credibility and trust.

Even those who swear by customer satisfaction, kneel at the altar of customer loyalty, and embrace the verbiage and the virtues of customer success abandon all principles the last day of the last month in the last quarter of the year.

Sadly, most of this was just customer "happy talk" — something to espouse and arouse, not enact and impact.

Dim Practice: No matter what they say, very few organizations live and breathe customer-centricity. And a make-you-sad, way-too-high percentage are customer clueless.

Want some proof? Organizations that operationalize customer intimacy are quite rare despite what their mission statements proclaim. Figure 1.1 demonstrates the findings of recent research — only 3% of 140 organizations studied were truly "cus-

FIGURE 1.1 Supplier-Customer Intimacy Meter

32%	65%	3%
OBLIVIOUS	NOW AND THEN	COMMITTED

tomer-centric," while fully one-third was found to be "customer-oblivious."[2] Yikes!

The ramifications of this important fact will be addressed in more detail later.

So, Alex, with that said, what makes you think that this "customer success thing" will actually change suppliers' attitudes toward customers?

For many organizations, customer success must be embraced as a full-body emersion, or they will endure a slow, painful death by drowning in the shallow end of the pool. The game has been changed, the ante has gone up, and the stakes are really high.

1. **Some organizations have no choice today.** If you are a subscription-based supplier with customers who have limited investment in you, low switching costs if they change to a different supplier, and little perceived risk in doing so, you will not survive without dutifully following the customer success model. Abandonment will rain down like hail in an Iowa cornfield in July. If you fall into this category and have no workable customer success model in place, you better call Customer-Success-Crisis-Line-911. Set this book down, dial now, and hope operators are waiting for your call.

2. **Most organizations will have no choice tomorrow.** Unless your offering is the diamond in the coal pile and your customers cannot flourish without it, changing customer attitudes and sophistication, and constantly improving technologies, mean that only those suppliers who help customers receive business outcomes, achieve personal wins, and provide a great customer experience while doing it, will win. Most of you reading this fall into this category. Avoid delay and begin today. You are burning daylight. Damn the torpedoes, full speed ahead.

But no worries. I will soon lay out the model—the dos and don'ts, the whys and the whens, and outline all the components of building a brilliant customer success organization. But first I want to point out the challenges your customer success peers face, and that you will probably face as well.

Most Important Customer Success Challenges

Respondents to my customer success study were quite forthcoming in outlining their most significant challenges.

Figure 1.2 represents the most important challenges research participant organizations faced when building customer success capabilities.

Figure 1.2 The Most Important Customer Success Issues

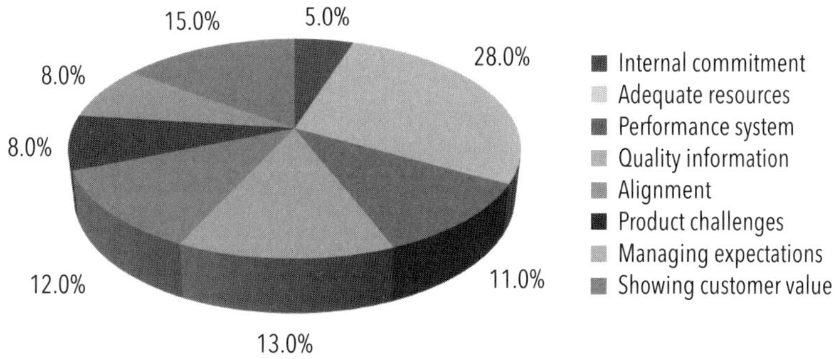

- Internal commitment
- Adequate resources
- Performance system
- Quality information
- Alignment
- Product challenges
- Managing expectations
- Showing customer value

28.0%, 5.0%, 15.0%, 8.0%, 8.0%, 12.0%, 13.0%, 11.0%

Internal Commitment
Although only 5% of the total responses fell into this category, the level of internal commitment (especially with organization executives) plays a big part in resource allocation and overcoming all of the other challenges groupings described.

As shown below in actual participant responses, understanding and committing to culture change are core requirements of effectively delivering customer success for organizations adding to or swapping their traditional model for a customer success model.

- *First and foremost is the company's commitment to customer success. Most seem to be creating it only because everyone else is doing it.*
- *We have to change the mindset at the company.*
- *The culture of the business making our customers the scapegoats.*
- *The understanding that customer success is everyone's responsibility, and that everyone can impact a customer's success.*

Adequate Resources

Whether begging ingredients for a lemonade stand or acquiring offshore rights for an energy company, obtaining resources is always an issue with new ventures, and this was true with the research respondents. About one-quarter of the issues in this category dealt with money—from budgeting to cash flow, to how to reduce cost, to influencing new sales. Obviously, available funding is a precursor to addressing the other resource issues described. Here are a few example comments.

Money
- *Budget.*
- *ROI cycle.*
- *Cash flow.*
- *Monetization of success.*

Talent

Over one-third of the responses dealt with talent, including hiring, developing, and retaining quality people. Representative comments include:
- *Finding industry vertical skills to match with product skills.*
- *Proper education of internal teams across the entire organization.*
- *Having enough resources to effectively handle all the needs of large clients on all fronts.*
- *Hire and retain the right people.*

Other Resource Issues

Other resource issues reported varied across the board. For example:
- *Scope of support.*
- *24x7 coverage, as follow the sun.*
- *Cover all languages.*
- *Programs that are scalable.*

Performance System

The performance system addresses the necessary elements required to make talent productive. Participants identified measures such as expectations, goals, and metrics needed to be defined, the appropriate structure for delivering customer success was either not in place or not working, and the need for robust processes were also mentioned as needed, but absent.

Measures
- *Determine what success means.*
- *Identify the main important goals.*
- *Metrics aren't well defined.*
- *Utilization metrics, early warning.*

Structure

Some comments talked about challenges in how they were organized:
- *Organization.*
- *Global structure.*
- *Reorganizing teams to support this new business function.*
- *Being single point for trusted contact after product installation.*

Processes

Going hand-in-hand with structure, several comments include:
- *We do not yet have all the processes and systems in place to support*

consistency in experience.
- *Define actions and the activities to meet the agreed goals.*
- *Defining internal working.*
- *We need a better approach to proactively preventing escalations.*

Quality Information

One could make the case that quality information belongs in the performance system category, but since so many responses related to information, it was established as a separate category. Here are some responses:
- *Data quality issues.*
- *Usage tracking for all products.*
- *Predictive analytics to find trends for incremental revenues.*
- *360-degree view on customer life cycle health, solution usage information, accurate customer contact information.*

As you know, quality information is always important to any entity. However, due to the time demands of customer success discussed later, getting quality information fast is mandatory in customer success.

Alignment

The main themes in this category were clear expectations of different functions' roles in delivering customer success, plus an emphasis on the need for collaboration. Responses included:
- *Cross-functional collaboration.*
- *Getting alignment with other organizations to make customer success.*
- *Making sure that you are leveraging your customer success resources across as many strategic customers as possible, without over-investing in any single customer.*
- *Executing with business partners.*
- *Prioritizing key customer issues above non-key customer issues in a way that no one customer feels slighted or ignored.*

- *Charter and segmentation for on-premise and cloud.*

Product Solution Challenges
Product quality and system stability were noted as making it harder to deliver customer success.
- *Poor product quality: a consistently poorly functioning product can strain a good relationship.*
- *Reduce the effort required to implement and use our products and solutions.*
- *System stability.*
- *How to keep our products sticky and in use.*

Managing Expectations
Setting, resetting, and managing customer expectations, and getting the customer to accept those expectations, were seen as critical issues for many participants.
- *Setting the right expectation.*
- *Gap between requirements versus promises versus delivery.*
- *Unreasonably high expectations.*
- *Gaining agreement on success criteria.*

Showing Customer Value
Comments in this category touch on the requirement to demonstrate value during all aspects of the customer buying and using processes. However, many comments directly mentioned or implied showed value during on-boarding.
- *On-boarding; successful experience determines overall lifetime.*
- *Aligning product usage and adoption to the achievement of internal and external business goals and objectives (value proposition).*
- *Perception of value; making sure customers understand the value of our products and services.*
- *The individuals using the program often have no idea what their company purchased. People are generally unaware of the benefits they are entitled to.*

Comparisons

When comparing the responses of on-site suppliers versus off-site suppliers there was very little difference. When comparing organizations with mature customer success capabilities versus those with less-mature capabilities, the mature organizations had fewer issues with regard to money, and somewhat fewer issues around alignment.

Chapter Summary

At this point we have identified the importance, the necessity, the realities, and the most common challenges to transitioning to customer success. For the remainder of the book, I will talk about what to do to fulfill the necessities, embrace the realities, and overcome the challenges in building brilliant customer success. Chapter 2 is all about creating brilliant customer experiences.

CHAPTER 2

Brilliant Customer Experiences

As defined in the Introduction, the customer experience is the customer's key player's perception of a supplier's performance, including activities that do not directly touch the key player but that affect her overall view of the supplier. Like customer success, customer experience is personal. As shown in Figure 2.1, brilliant customer experiences enable the supplier to help the customer get what they want, the way they want it.

Figure 2.1 Brilliant Customer Experiences Enable Customer Success

A customer state of mind in which she feels she has achieved her desires (business outcomes and personal wins) while undergoing brilliant customer experiences.

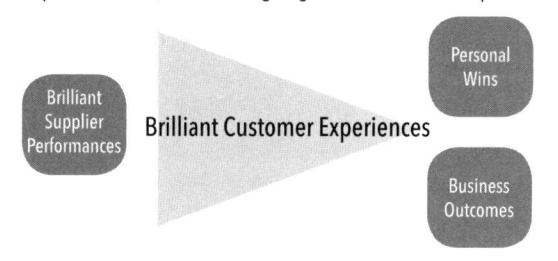

So let's start this conversation by looking at what you need to do to deliver on the seven things that your customers want, expect, and deserve, as seen in Figure 2.2.

Figure 2.2 The 7 Things Your Customers Want, Expect, and Deserve

	Never　　　　　　　　　　Always
1. Deliver on the promise	1 2 3 4 5 6 7 8 9 10
2. Transparency	1 2 3 4 5 6 7 8 9 10
3. No hassle	1 2 3 4 5 6 7 8 9 10
4. Responsiveness	1 2 3 4 5 6 7 8 9 10
5. Evidence you care	1 2 3 4 5 6 7 8 9 10
6. Fairness	1 2 3 4 5 6 7 8 9 10
7. Control	1 2 3 4 5 6 7 8 9 10

Brilliant Customer Experiences: The Seven Things Your Customers Want, Expect, and Deserve[1]

1. Deliver on the promise.

As cowboys in the Old West movies often stated, "Your word is your bond." The customer wants, expects, and deserves that you do what you said you will do, when, where, and how it was promised. Your reliability and credibility are on the line. So slow down, think, explore, confirm, check, and think again before you make a commitment. Remember that delivering customer success is a team event, and you have many cooks making the customer stew. Everyone needs to embrace and live by this principle.

2. Transparency.

Nobody likes surprises, especially when addressing important issues. Neglecting to discuss a few items that the customer may not like, or allowing your lawyers to put in pages of non-customer-friendly fine print in a contract that negates what the customer thinks or what your commitment states are not best practices! Be crystal-clear about what will happen, what won't happen, and what might happen. Act like a trusted advisor and share the whole picture—explain the bad along with the good. And, of course, don't lie (what would your grandmother think?). Besides, people always find out, and people never forget.

3. No hassle.
Your customers should not dread the thought of attempting to get what they want from your organization, and then agonize and struggle to get it. Waiting on hold forever while a recording keeps repeating how important they are, asking them to provide information that your company should already have or that is irrelevant, and not being able to communicate with competent people all take a toll on the customer—one they should not have to pay. Let them communicate with you how they want to communicate with you. Make it easy to buy, easy to access information, and easy to get service and support.

4. Responsiveness.
Customers want fast reactions to inquiries and timely resolution of issues. Is that too much to ask?

5. Evidence you care.
Customers are much more understanding of your situation and your feelings when they believe you understand their situation and care about their feelings. So stop, listen, and empathize with the customer before moving on to business. Evidencing you care is especially vital when you mess up and the customer knows you messed up. They want to know why things went south, what you are going to do about it, and they expect (and deserve) an apology. Man up when you mess up, and fix the customer first.

6. Fairness.
Most customers have a realistic understanding of what fairness is

in any situation. Most don't expect "Wow!" experiences, nor do they want their socks blown off. Ninety-eight percent of customers do not try to take advantage of suppliers who they perceive are trying to act fairly. Don't let your legal or financial people skew your practices and policies to protect against the 2 percent of customers who are the bad eggs. Empower your frontline personnel to do what is right.

7. Control.
Customers often feel that once they sign on with a supplier, they have little choice as to what will happen and how it will happen. Resentment builds when the supplier drives the car and appears to ignore the customer sitting in the backseat. Customers want to control the supplier-customer relationship — control in how they buy, control in getting information, and control when getting service. So don't dictate that the customer follow your agenda; always give customers choices when decisions are required.

OK, the above is not hard to understand. I bet it is exactly what you want, expect, and feel you deserve when you are in the role of customer.

As I am sure you noticed, Figure 2.2 is in an assessment format. It can be a simple yet powerful tool to get the attention of the nonbelievers in your organization. The instructions for the Hassle Meter described later in this chapter would apply to this assessment as well. You have my permission to copy and to use either or both of these tools.

What Does the Customer Get?

Now that we know the universal seven things that all customers want, expect, and deserve, how does your organization measure up? Chances are high that your organization's overall customer experience is worse than you think. For example, while 80 percent of executives in a recent study proclaimed their organizations deliver excellent customer experiences, when the customers of these executives where asked, only 8 percent said they received an excellent customer experience[2]...isn't it scary that so many senior managers live in La-La Land? Is customer experience fairy dust sprinkled in your boardroom?

Dim Practice: Not testing your assumptions.

The Implications of Poor Customer Experience[3]

Like spilling red wine on the Queen's new carpet, the implications of poor customer experiences can be huge, both outside and inside the organization.

Outside the organization:
- **Disloyalty.** A negative customer experience reduces customer loyalty by an average of 20 percent.
- **Lost customers.** Normally, half of all customer attrition is voluntary and due to poor customer experiences.
- **Brand damage.** There is a much higher probability of bad press, law suits, and negative word of mouth when customers have bad experiences.
- **Pricing pressure.** Customer sensitivity to price increases significantly when problems occur, often doubling on the initial occurrence and doubling again with multiple problem occurrences.

Inside the organization:
- **Wasted effort.** Most companies could prevent 30 percent of service contacts with better communication up front.
- **Lower employee morale.** Your employees don't like working for a loser. When your organization does stupid or irrational things it impacts their mindset and their actions.

Customer Experience Realities[4]

Below are the most important realities of customer experience management:

1. Based upon the above sections on "What the Customer Gets" and the "Implications of Poor Customer Experience," it is highly likely that your customers' experiences are needlessly leaving huge amounts of money on the table.
2. Service does not own the customer experience. Support does not own it. Sales does not own it. Everyone owns it.
3. Understanding and then setting, resetting, managing, and meeting customer expectations is much harder to do than most people think.
4. Employees do not cause most customer dissatisfaction, your processes and your procedures are the biggest culprits.
5. No news is usually bad news; a company receiving few complaints is not always delivering a great customer experience. Only one-third and, more likely, one-twelfth of customers call the company about a problem.
6. Technology has changed what customers expect from a company and how the company delivers the customer experience.
7. Comparing yourself to best-in-class organizations is no longer enough. Customers compare their experience with you against the best experiences they have ever had. Hence, "best practices" make sense to measure your customer success performance against when you are just starting, but "distinguishing practices" should be your guide as you mature.
8. It is a fact that good service does not necessarily equate to a great overall customer experience. Often the customer correctly feels that the problem should never have occurred in the first place.
9. Customers are willing to forgive manufacturing or operational mistakes, but they will not forgive being intentionally misled. It is not in the DNA of the sales and marketing departments

to set proper expectations. They tend to stress the positive attributes of the product and deemphasize (or totally ignore) its limitations and weaknesses. When the sales or marketing departments fail to clearly communicate product limitations, they are creating dissatisfaction of the worst kind.

The Two Contributors to Brilliant Customer Experiences

There are two contributors that create brilliant customer experiences:
1. **Do it right the first time.** Consistent, appropriate, positive actions.
2. **Do it very right the second time.** Send champagne with the roses.

1. Do It Right the First Time (DIRTFT): Consistent, Appropriate, Positive Actions

When you want to be dependable,
Make your offerings vendible,
Focus with persistence…always be consistent,
And the results will be commendable.

The desired result, of course, of DIRTFT is to achieve hassle-free customer success. So, starting with your must-have customers, plan, prepare, and perform.

1. **Stir the Pot.** Engage key people to gain momentum. Follow the instructions you will read about under the Hassle Meter. This will engage, intrigue, and possibly shame, but probably motivate your key internal players to aggressively address improving your customer experience. Using that momentum…
2. **Map the Moments.** Create/enhance touchpoint maps for

your must-have segment. Put together a team to lay out all the moments of truth between your customers and your business. Yes, you want people with knowledge of all of the six major touchpoints, but include some other smart people that don't have that customer interaction expertise. They will be valuable for the next step:

    a. Start with "ideal." This is dream time. Don't let the past fog a possible future. Keep your most experienced people from saying "we tried that" or "there is no way that will work." Come up with an elegant solution—simple, easy, impactful.

    b. Next, determine the "is." This is established from the customer's perspective, starting with how the customer hears about, buys, takes delivery, and uses your offering. In this map, you then build in all the touches the customer has with your organization and any channel partners or distributors.

    c. Establish a "should be" touchpoint map. Based upon the realities at hand, agree upon a move-ahead "should be" map. Fight every additional contact that does not add value—often, less is more. Keep as close to the ideal map as your situation allows.

3. **Define and Align.** Implement technology to provide your customer-facing personnel with what they need, when they need it, as determined by Step 2.
4. **Customize by Account (as appropriate).**
5. **Track, Measure, Adjust.**

Much more on mapping will follow in Chapter 5.

The Hassle Meter
Thinking back to Step 1, Stir the Pot, I suggest using the Hassle Meter to kick-start positive customer success behaviors in your organization.

I introduced the concept of "no hassle" earlier in outlining the seven things that customers want, expect, and deserve. However, it is such an important contributor to non-brilliant customer experience, it deserves its own section.

Figure 2.3 poses the question: How easy are you to do business with (ETDBW)? As noted in the previous section, here is a simple, yet powerful, tool to find the answer and open up some eyes for the need for touchpoint mapping. Let me suggest how to use it.

Figure 2.3 The Hassle Meter: How Easy Is Your Company to Do Business With?

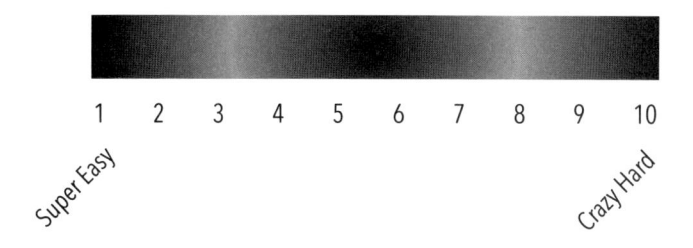

Get the Inside Perception
1. In a group setting, hand out copies of the Hassle Meter to your team (and/or other teams and/or your executives), and ask each person to circle the number they feel your customers would select to rate your organization on how easy you are to do business with. You can discuss customers overall, choose your five newest customers, or select designated major accounts—whatever you feel would be most valuable.
2. Next, ask them to jot down on the form at least three reasons why they selected that number.
3. Discuss and record the responses, and note the similarities and differences.

By itself, this is a simple way to generate meaningful thought and conversation about the customer experience, which is valuable in its own right. However, don't stop there. Get the team to agree to validate their thinking by listening to the voice of the customer.

Find the Outside Reality
4. Visit the customers you referenced in Step 1, hand them the Hassle Meter, and ask them to give you a candid score.
5. After they complete this step, ask them for reasons why they scored you as they did and to please share examples that demonstrate those reasons. Let them talk, encourage them to expand.
6. After thanking them for their candid input, ask them for suggestions as to how to make things better and, of course, record those recommendations.

Take Action
7. Share the findings with the people inside your organization who took part in Step 1 and compare the inside perception with the outside reality (I'd suggest a half-day session). Be prepared for some verbal denial, frowned faces, and signs of stomach pains. This dose of reality may feel like a bucket full of ice water over the head to some. Once the group has quieted down, identify the common issues, do some root-cause analysis and brainstorming, and then come up with some specific actions you commit to take to be easier to do business with. This is a great way to make meaningful improvement. But don't stop there!
8. Revisit each customer you met with earlier, share your findings, and explain the actions you are taking based upon customer feedback. Customers are used to having suppliers seek their input, but NO ONE EVER COMES BACK OR MAKES MEANINGFUL CHANGES based on the input collected! They will be shocked. They will be awed. A few will

be open to helping you help them and be part of the team I recommended in Step 7.
9. Taking the time (and maybe the hassle) to return to your customers with your findings will distinguish you from the pack, and you will be seen (and remembered) as the caring, committed customer experience professional you are.

DIRTFTs first cousin is repeatability—consistently doing things the right way, which is the dream of all those who head operations. Once the touchpoint maps are made, the goal is to consistently apply those actions again and again.

Relentless Repeatability
When asked what is the key to mastery, Ben Hogan, one of the greatest golfers of all time summed it up in just two words, "relentless repeatability." The context of his response, of course, was related to a simple, consistent golf swing. Yet here is advice that aligns very nicely to everyone tasked with delivering brilliant customer experiences. Let me explain.

- **Repeatability and trust.** Almost all of us would like to be seen, and have our people be seen, as trusted advisors. Not only do business economics demonstrate the value of attaining this, but personally it also is extremely fulfilling to be seen in that special role. Whether with customers, teammates, friends, or family, one of the key drivers of creating trust is reliability—consistently fulfilling promises time and time again.[5] There is one stroke for the benefits of repeatability.
- **Repeatability and branding credibility.** Want to make a marketer drool? Show him how your prime prospects will hear the same great news about you in the same way over and over and over. No one likes surprises (at least in business), and the power of repeatability is its ability to create credibility in the marketplace by mastering your market message.

- **Repeatability and quality.** Another way to think of repeatability is the old quality concept of "doing it right the first time, over and over again." When this occurs, rework is minimized for you, and hassle is minimized for your customers—a classic win-win scenario.[6]
- **Repeatability and growth.** The ability to ramp up frontline capability is a requirement (and often a major headache) in attaining profitable growth. Robust processes routinely followed by appropriately skilled people are the basis of scalability. Repeatability scores again.

Relentless repeatability—only two words, but what a powerful purpose statement. Adapt it as your own mantra and watch your performance ignite.

2. Do It Very Right the Second Time: Send Champagne with the Roses

When things go down the slippery slope,
Don't hesitate, procrastinate, or mope.
Speed your reaction,
Jump into action,
And the results will be more than you hope.

One of the most powerful credibility drivers available to organizations comes from a situation most of us dread: screw-ups—the implementation that never worked or the problem fix that never stuck. The things that result in a hassle for you and a headache for your customer are marvelous opportunities to turn chicken feathers into chicken soup.

Yet, even execs with a lifetime of dealing with (and solving) tough customer problems often blow their chance in handling a not-so-great customer experience. They (like all of us) are subconsciously attracted to adopting problem-avoidance tactics

aimed at "minimizing damage" instead of embracing the relationship-building opportunities to "maximize the value" that problems naturally create. See if these three problem-avoidance approaches sound familiar:
1. Reject: "It doesn't sound like a big deal to me. You can't expect something to work 100 percent of the time, can you?"
Or …
2. Ignore: "Maybe if we don't do anything, the problem will fix itself. Let's allow this to sit awhile and see what happens."
Or …
3. Disagree: "No, it is not our fault—this is complex stuff! Customers are always trying to blame us when the root cause lies in something they did wrong."

These attitudes drive behaviors that have a very similar impact on the customer experience. Whenever customers face screw-ups they feel two things: a sense of loss and a sense of dread—loss, in that they did not get what they paid for (expectations not met), and dread, at the thought of having to go through the hassle of attempting to get the supplier to "do what is right." Past experience has taught them that supplier problems of any kind are often a major pain to resolve.

Think about your personal history with supplier problems. Remember how you felt (after leaving three voicemails) when trying to get the contractor who "fixed" your roof to come out and repair the roof when it still leaked? How confident were you of getting a timely resolution? Or recall how you felt on the third visit to the dealership when the car mechanic smugly said, "I don't hear any clunking noise at 50 miles an hour. You are just hearing the clock."

How did you feel when your viewpoint was dismissed and it was inferred that you were an imbecile? I'm sure you can come up with many more examples, but the feelings are the same: a sense of loss and a sense of dread as our patterns of customer experiences prepare us for agony and toil. These are not pleasant feelings!

Your customers feel exactly the same way when facing service problems caused by or related to your offerings.

Making Chicken Soup Out of Chicken Feathers

Every time you follow the all-too-common path of rejecting, ignoring, or disagreeing, you lose an enormous opportunity to provide a wonderful experience that helps create a loyal customer. People are so used to being rejected out of hand, ignored when they complain, and disagreed with when they offer ideas, that they are absolutely amazed when they are met with understanding, accountability, and action. Furthermore, if your empowered customer success team handles a problem with a service recovery approach, customers will be impressed and delighted with not only your actions, but also with you and your entire organization as well. They will tell others about the brilliant customer experience. They will become very valuable assets. So pay attention, as this can directly impact your success. Here is what you need to do.

Develop a Brilliant Service Recovery Approach

Rethink your whole approach toward dealing with customer problems. Don't hide behind old rules—throw them out and start over:

1. Change your mindset from "oh, cripes, another problem to deal with" to "sorry it happened, but what a great opportunity!"
2. Change your problem-resolution strategy from "what is the minimum we can do to get by" to a service recovery strategy of "what is the best way to fix the problem so it stays fixed and creates a loyal customer?"
3. Change a core metric from "overall customer satisfaction" to

"number of champions (very loyal customers) created."

Like most important things, you'll improve both quality and buy-in if you involve your team in crafting your service recovery approach.

Create a Brilliant Service Recovery Process

Figure 2.4 shows the five foundations of powerful service recovery. Read on, and you'll see that they are not only a process to be followed, but also a philosophy to be lived.

Figure 2.4 The 5 Foundations of Service Recovery

1	'Fess up when you mess up.
2	Make no excuses.
3	Have a need for speed.
4	Pass out the capes and unload the bus.
5	Send champagne with the roses.

1. 'Fess up when you mess up.
This is all about the person who is on the spot, whatever his or her rank, assuming full and immediate accountability for full problem resolution when you or your company's actions are the cause of the problem. This means no arguing about who is to blame. No "I have to check with my supervisor" and no "our escalation policy is…."

The person is empowered to start turning the crank of service recovery immediately. No permission is needed. (You have a service recovery strategy, remember?) Fixing the problem with a solution that will last is job number one. Communicate that your only concern is fixing the problem. You can worry about all the other stuff later. Expect open mouths and other signs of disbelief from your customer's staff. (If you're pretty darn certain the problem isn't your doing, read "But What If It's Not Our Fault" at the end of this chapter.)

2. Make no excuses.
If you screwed up, eat some humble pie and apologize. Forget about what your legal department may say about never admitting failure in order to avoid liability. That is sheer stupidity. You are dealing with people who deserve honesty and respect. If the customer knows you screwed up, and you know you screwed up, and the customer knows you know you screwed up, then 'fess up when you mess up. It is an insult to the customer's staff members if you don't apologize when they deserve an apology.

If you are not sure if you screwed up (or are sure you didn't), then empathize. Let everyone know you understand their problem and its implications. Yes, there are facts to be dealt with, but deal with the feelings first. This personal listening/understanding/connecting goes a long way in cooling down a hot situation.

3. Have a need for speed.
You are now being watched closely to see if your words are for real or just BS. People at the customer's organization want to believe you, but past experience makes them skeptical. So have a need for speed. Quit burning daylight. Damn the torpedoes! Full speed ahead! Just do it.

Light a fire under whomever you need to get action started. Send the customer a daily report (more or less often, depending on the situation) outlining what your organization has done today to address the problem, the results thus far, and what next steps are planned. This report could go to one or more people. Then phone a representative for the customer to explain, and respond to the problem (apologize and empathize again, as required).

4. Pass out the capes and unload the bus.
Remember that this is your chance to turn a lump of coal into a diamond. Bring in your big hitters, whether Geeks or Suits (doughnuts and pizza also help). When you ring the bell of service recovery, the best and the brightest should now be available. (Remember, you have a service recovery strategy.) This is the role that your service people love to play, so hype up the situation and give them the opportunity to shine like the stars they are.

5. Send champagne with the roses.
Here is the "awe" your customer will experience. You resolved the problem to meet original expectations and fixed the root cause, so the hydra of hassle won't raise its ugly head(s) again. On top of doing it fast and with style, one more thing you need to do is to delight—to awe them.

Here is a personal example many readers may relate to: If you make a blunder like being out of town on work at the time of your anniversary, your significant other may "expect," along with a "geez, I'm sorry," a small token, such as flowers or candy. So sending a dozen or two long-stemmed (red or yellow, I forget) roses may exceed those expectations. Sounds like a smart move! Can you anticipate the reaction?

What about the reaction received by a very small few (the brilliant) among us who also send two bottles of champagne with a note saying something like, "Please ice this down and we can share it together tomorrow night." This kind of behavior is totally unexpected...something to be remembered...something that makes you unique in an important person's eyes.

That is what we are talking about. It is not asking, "What can we do to make this right?" It is just doing it—discovering something else of value that you can provide and making it so. What reaction do you expect now? Going a little further, doing a little more, forms a story that will not be forgotten. Plus, it is satisfying and fun. Remember: It only costs a little more to go first class, and important people, like your customers (and loved ones), deserve it.

Excite and Empower Your Team

Explain your service recovery strategy to everyone who touches the customer. Communicate that it is everyone's responsibility to launch service recovery. Train them on the skills, coach them on the process, and explain the value. Provide real-world examples of customer problems, ranging from customer irritants to full-blown train wrecks, in order to link concepts to reality. Have people play themselves in role-plays of how they would handle service recovery. Have managers coach them to think "extreme" in considering how to turn a hassle into an awesome customer experience. Your team will love it.

If you can discipline yourself and your organization to get past old thinking and procedures regarding customer problems, you can use service recovery to gain a unique position in your marketplace, create customer loyalty, and have a bunch of fun doing it. Why not start today?

But What If It's Not Our Fault?

Sometimes customers point the finger of fault at you when you know there is no or little probability that the problem was caused by you. Don't pass it off, take advantage of this situation by finding some way to help without taking improper ownership. A statement expressing your desire to help goes a long way in demonstrating your customer-driven philosophy. Here's an example:

"Mr. Customer, based upon what you said, I think the problem may lie elsewhere. However, root-cause analysis can be determined later. What is most important is getting your issue resolved as easily as possible. May I put you in contact with XX at

Y? She is an expert in this area and may have some suggestions. Also, while we have been talking, I emailed you an article that might be useful."

Chapter Summary

This chapter started with outlining the seven things that all customers want, expect, and deserve. This is your customer experience scorecard. Next, I pointed out that often this is not what the customer gets, along with the probable bad impacts this can have for you as a supplier. I then shared some realities for you to ponder. From there I provided the overarching goal of doing it right the first time, and provided a Hassle Meter to stir the pot and turn the crank on customer experience. However, stuff happens, and instead of moaning and complaining, take advantage of the situation by doing things very right the second time. Finally, empowering your people to do the appropriate thing occasionally as the opportunity arises, and sending champagne with the roses can yield a very big impact for a tiny investment in time and money.

Speaking of your people, now it is time to learn what it takes to deliver brilliant customer experiences.

Note: This chapter was inspired by and borrows heavily from the work of John Goodman, especially his book Customer Experience 3.0: High Profit Strategies in the Age of Techno Service *(AMACOM. 2014). I highly recommend all those interested in learning more about customer experience to tap into this excellent resource.*

CHAPTER 3

Brilliant Employees

For the customer to have brilliant experiences, brilliant employee performances are required at every step. Performing brilliantly requires employees that are not only highly capable, but who are also enabled and motivated to deliver their best. Loyalty to your company and its customer-centered mission is a core requirement of consistently delivering that success over time and in sometimes-challenging situations.

I will start with the traditional skill sets and core capabilities of conventional marketing, sales, and service professionals, and then discuss the additional attributes needed in the delivery of brilliant customer success.

I know that some readers might take exception to calling marketing a part of the customer success frontline team. However, their actions have such an important impact during moments of truth that I chose to include them here and in later chapters.

From Traditional Frontline Personnel to Brilliant Customer Success Team

Past research I conducted demonstrates a significant transformation occurring in the world of customer-facing personnel over the last twenty years. More customers and suppliers are understanding the big impact that these professionals have on improving the customer experience and delivering customer success when they expand their role. When customer-facing personnel behave in the suggested way described shortly, there is a direct linkage to stronger customer relationships, increased sales, and deeper customer loyalty. Figure 3.1 shows the prime components of this transformation.

Figure 3.1 From Traditional Frontline Personnel to Brilliant Customer Success Team

REACTIVE	+	PROACTIVE
TACTICAL	+	STRATEGIC
CONTROL	+	COLLABORATE
VALUE ADDER	+	VALUE CREATOR
TECHNICAL ACUMEN	+	CUSTOMER ACUMEN
PROFESSIONAL TRUST	+	PERSONAL TRUST
GOOD COMMUNICATION SKILLS	⟶	GREAT COMMUNICATION SKILLS

Reactive + Proactive
Marketing
In most organizations that follow the traditional model, marketers react to the trends and issues of the marketplace defined by others (e.g., McKinsey, Accenture, IBM). They attempt to be early adopters as they align their value proposition and marketing messages as best they can.

In the customer success approach, marketers are reactive as necessary, but their focus is to touch key potential customers much earlier in the decision process. They strive to be viewed by their marketplace as thought leaders, hence they conduct their own original research, publish white papers, host forums, speak at conferences, and mingle with the other movers and shakers in their industry.

Sales
Traditionally the salesperson waits for leads to come in from marketing campaigns and jumps on them with a vengeance. However, by the time the lead hits the inbox, the customer (possibly influenced by a competitor) has already defined the requirements of their intended solution, causing the seller to have to react and adjust to the standards already in place. Opportunity lost. Worse, the lead may never arrive, as a competitor may have swept in and you never even knew about it.

In the customer success approach, sellers (helped by marketing opening the door) make contact with the prospective customer earlier in the decision-making process, allowing them the opportunity to help shape the issues and the possible solutions, while at the same time starting important relationships. This early bird approach greatly increases the probability of getting the worm (the new sales).

Service
For most service pros, much of their time is spent being reactive, addressing the issues and solving the problems brought to their attention by the customer or by their sales colleagues. When the alarm rings, they slide down the pole, jump into their boots, and hustle off to put out the fire. It is critical that these challenges continue to be addressed both effectively and efficiently, however, the proactive service pro seizes the initiative and aggressively looks for ways to prevent problems and find new oppor-

tunities that will benefit the customer. Proactive service pros are not afraid to challenge existing standards and explore new ways of thinking.

Tactical + Strategic
Does your customer success team need to be in the weeds sometimes? Of course. Slicing and dicing quantitative market information, explaining the intricate differences among various options, tracking usage of key customer users during on-boarding, and so on, are all important, must-do tasks.

However, the customer success team also needs also to be strategic—to look at the big picture, know the customer road map, focus on the future of the account, and recommend fresh ideas on how he can have the biggest customer impact.

Control + Collaborate
When facing time-sensitive customer issues, it is often best for a customer success team member to take control to just "git 'er done." But the customer success team realizes that significant positive change requires collaboration. Their mindset is to put the customer first, and then align plans and actions so that the customer and your company and the customer success team all win. Attempting change without participation is like trying to make bread without the yeast—it won't rise to the occasion.

Value Adder + Value Creator
Responding to issues quickly and effectively, and then communicating the benefit to the customer in a professional manner, adds value. However, proactively and strategically developing innovative recommendations that are accepted by the customer has the potential to add new value. Acting as a business advisor, customer success team members aggressively look for these opportunities and challenge the customer's views whether they are asked to or not.

Technical Acumen + Customer Acumen

Solid technical knowledge is vital to delivering customer success, but as long as it exists within the team, not everyone has to be technically strong. For example, team members whose main task is to get the business need to be able to talk technology at a high level, but can then rely on others to deal with customer geeks. Technical acumen is a given; it is table stakes to play the game. But customer acumen—having a very solid knowledge of the customer's business, their industry, their marketplace, and business in general is a potential way to differentiate yourself. Your strong sellers are probably already solid in customer acumen, but the more everyone else can speak the customer's language, the better the possibility to influence customers to move forward.

Professional Trust + Personal Trust

Your frontline people earn professional trust by applying their knowledge and skills to effectively and efficiently fulfill their roles, e.g., delivering helpful information and solving customer problems quickly and professionally.

The brilliant customer success team goes a step further, however, by earning the personal trust of their customers. When customers know you have their back, they are much more open to confidently take steps they perceive as bigger risks.

From Good to Great Communication Skills

Behaving brilliantly requires that your team go beyond having good communication skills. They work, hone, and sharpen the core skills that result in great relationship building. In fact, the executives in my past research stated that this is the most important differentiator between their stars and everyone else. For example, in the last decade or so, progressive services and support leaders have been turning to their frontline personnel (field service engineers, support account managers, professional services consultants, and so on) to:

58 | BRILLIANT EMPLOYEES

- Deepen trust-based relationships with key customers,
- Gain more business in existing accounts, and thereby
- Create competitive advantage.

Lots of new knowledge, new skills, and new ways of thinking are needed, however, Figure 3.2 from my customer success study shows the five most important capabilities required of the frontline customer success team.

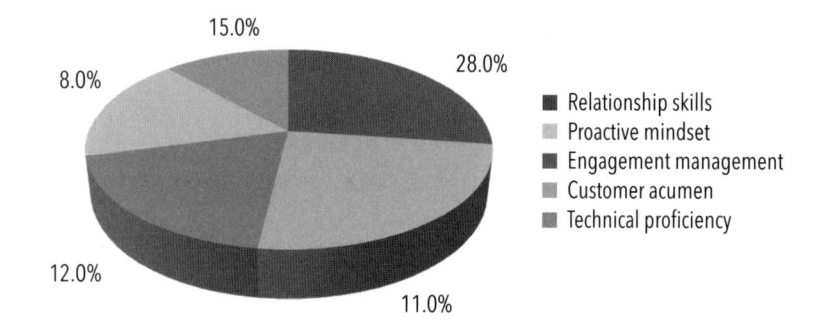

Figure 3.2 The 5 Capabilities Required of the Customer Success Team

- Relationship skills: 28.0%
- Proactive mindset: 15.0%
- Engagement management: 8.0%
- Customer acumen: 12.0%
- Technical proficiency: 11.0%

Relationship Skills

Many research participants spoke in broad terms about relationship skills, using words such as communication skills, relationship building, and soft skills. Others zeroed in on particular aspects of relationship building, such as trust building, listening, empathy, and influencing. About one-half of the relationship skills comments were focused inside the organization, such as good internal collaboration, orchestrating initiatives, rallying proper resources within the company, and navigating internal teams.

Proactive Mindset

Describers of a proactive mindset included comments such as

always looking for ways to improve the customer experience, adaptability to change, the foresight to recognize and hold off potential problems before they occur, innovative, and boldness to push for action.

Engagement Management
Terms included organization skills, project management, accountability, analytical skills, and managing competing priorities—all aspects of engagement management.

Customer Acumen
In their comments, participants confirmed the three components of customer acumen as having a good knowledge of (1) how customers make decisions, (2) the industry in which they operate, and (3) business in general.

Technical Proficiency
Research respondents talked about the importance of technical proficiency, including product expertise and technology competence.

Comparison: Cloud versus Everyone Else

In comparing subscription-only companies to everyone else, there were no differences.

The organizations that were more mature had a greater emphasis on relationship skills and customer acumen, with less emphasis on engagement management and technical proficiency than less mature organizations.

Findings from the Study

- Many questioned whether they had the correct talent to deliver customer success consistently.

- In many organizations, there are role and responsibility disconnects that add waste and confusion.
- The frontline requirements of delivering customer success are well known. An earlier study of mine defined these same five capabilities, and these requirements are the same as those required of frontline personnel implementing strategic account management. Hence, there is much experience in developing these qualities and capabilities.
- These frontline requirements of delivering customer success are the same for both suppliers operating under a traditional model or a subscription model.
- However, the depth of the capabilities required at each stage in the model (described later) varies with regard to who from the team should be tasked with doing it.

Figure 3.3 graphically explains that to get the desired results, the team must possess the five capabilities. To possess the five capabilities, both quality training and ongoing reinforcement needs to be in place.

Figure 3.3 Building New Capabilities: Creating Sustainable Performance

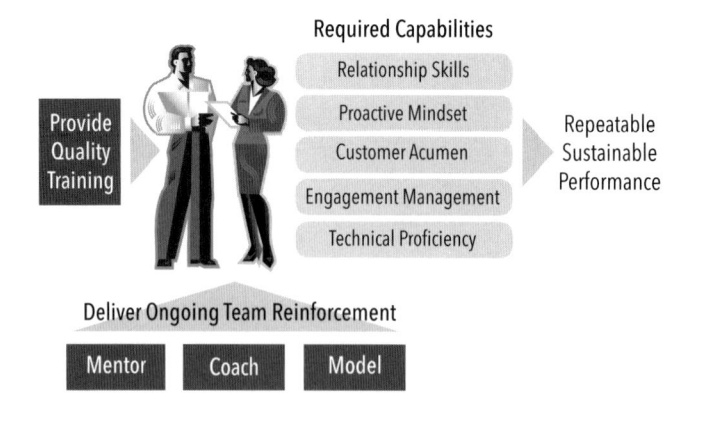

Recommendations

- In most all situations, delivering customer success requires a team approach. Hence, don't label an individual as a "customer success manager," as multiple people have a hand in the process.
- Train all members of the customer success team together on the same core skills described above.
- Realize that for many traditional organizations, the significant change in new ways of thinking and acting is a big deal. It is very important that along with quality training, management and team members mentor, coach, and model personnel on the new expectations.
- To speed and smooth the building of your customer success team capabilities, assess your current standing against what you want. This input will help focus the training and reinforcement efforts to maximize results.

Whiner Concern: "What if I spend a lot of money on training my customer success team and they all leave?"
Correct Response: "What if you don't train them and they all stay?"

Chapter Summary

The five competencies outlined above are the same five competencies defined in a study authored earlier defining the requirements of becoming a trusted advisor: customer acumen, relationship skills, proactive mindset, engagement management, and technical proficiency. As will be emphasized later in this book, these capabilities are required of the customer success team, and the percentage of each capability will vary by specific role and by specific process step. In order to enable these capabilities, brilliant performance systems must be in place.

CHAPTER 4

Brilliant Performance Systems

I don't care if your team has the smarts of Einstein and Bach, the personality of the Dallas cheerleaders, and the drive of presidential politicians, they will never be successful if a poor performance system is in place within your organization. For your employees to perform brilliantly, they must have robust, high-quality performance systems to support their efforts.

In general, a performance system is anything and everything your organization provides that helps employees consistently do their job the right way at the right time (relentless repeatability).

All aspects of your company can come into play in enabling your organization to deliver customer success. Obviously, product development is integral to the success of any company, and other functions ranging from HR to purchasing have an influence in how your people act and the impact on the customer.

However, as I did in the last chapter, I will focus on the three most important performance systems to overall success, which are robust quality in marketing, sales, and service.

Also in the previous chapter I stated that quality training and ongoing reinforcement were necessary requirements to putting the five customer success team capabilities into action.

Figure 4.1 adds the final core ingredient of a performance system—performance levers. The performance levers necessary to guide, encourage, and reward performance include:

- Clear expectations.
- Appropriate tools to do the job.
- Meaningful metrics that matter and motivate.[1]
- Consequences that reward a job well done and chide a job poorly done.
- Ongoing feedback on individual and team performance.
- Effective, efficient, and adaptive processes.

Figure 4.1 Brilliant Performance Systems

Adjust Performance Levers
Expectations
Tools
Metrics
Consequences
Feedback
Processes

Provide Quality Training

Required Capabilities
Relationship Skills
Proactive Mindset
Customer Acumen
Engagement Management
Technical Proficiency

Repeatable Sustainable Performance

Deliver Ongoing Team Reinforcement
Mentor | Coach | Model

When you adopt customer success as your strategy and your business model, you need to adjust existing performance systems to better meet your new criteria.

Structured Functions to Fluid Processes

In most organizations, customer-facing personnel are attached to a function: marketers to marketing, sellers to sales, and servicers to services. Lots of good things can come from this organizing structure, as it allows for specialization and clear lines of responsibility. However, efforts to drive efficiency often create friction, at best, and dysfunction, at worst, when goals, incentives, and ways of thinking are at cross purposes. The "process people" call this suboptimization—for example, sales administration might lower its operating costs by firing all sales support personnel and require the salespeople to do their own reporting. However, when one thinks about it, that is a stupid idea...taking a highly paid professional and having them do volumes of paperwork instead of high-value selling. Duh. Give the paperwork to the experts that know how to compile, slice, and dice data into meaningful information.

The challenge is to keep the good, and circumvent the natural friction that develops between and among departments. Hence, if you are becoming a customer-focused organization, you should align your business development processes to the customers' decision-making processes.

Customer Success Approach

A customer success supplier takes a different approach. Before elaborating the appropriate actions that the supplier should take when customer success is the prime objective, the supplier should first understand how the customer makes decisions. Once understood, the supplier can then align brilliant employee performances that deliver brilliant customer experiences and that lead to success as the customer defines it.

Figure 4.2 displays the six steps of the process that customers follow when making important decisions.

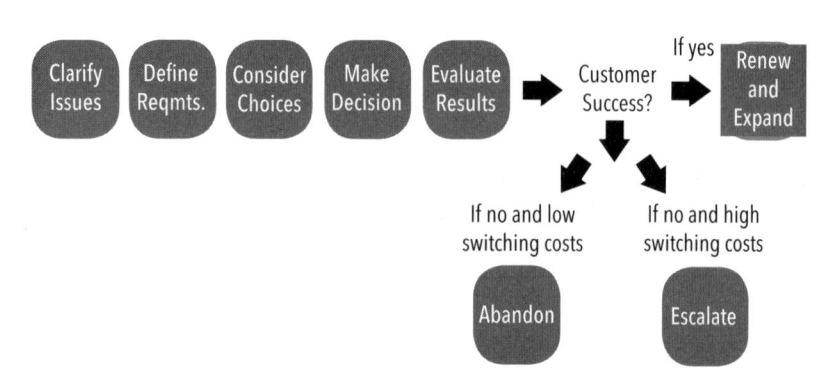

Figure 4.2 The Customer Decision-Making Process

```
Clarify → Define → Consider → Make → Evaluate → Customer  If yes → Renew
Issues   Reqmts.  Choices    Decision Results   Success?           and Expand
                                                    ↓  ↓
                                    If no and low    If no and high
                                    switching costs  switching costs
                                        Abandon         Escalate
```

1. **Clarifying issues.** Based upon the customer's organization strategy (blueprint), step one is clarifying issues, identifying the high-impact problems or opportunities that have the possibility of delivering or not delivering the results needed for meeting the goals of the customer blueprint, and that help bring about customer success.
2. **Defining requirements.** Once an issue is identified and deemed worthy to act upon, the customer defines requirements and outlines the desired results within specified boundaries of quality, cost, and time. Other boundary considerations may include ease of implementation, political consequences, etc.
3. **Considering choices.** With a clear understanding of requirements, choices are considered, and a shortlist of options is developed.
4. **Making decisions.** The decision might include doing nothing, postponing action, tackling the issue internally, or purchasing an offering from an outside supplier. For our purposes, the assumption is that an offering will be purchased from an external supplier.
5. **Evaluating results.** Evaluating starts immediately after the decision is made, but ultimately comes down to how well

key people within the customer feel their business outcomes and personal wins have been met and how satisfied they are with their experience with the supplier.
6. **Renewing and expanding.** If the results are perceived as poor, and switching costs are low, the customer may decide to abandon the offering purchased or the project in place and go with a different supplier. The more stake the customer has in the decision (the higher the switching costs), the more the customer may decide to escalate an unsatisfactory situation and open negotiations with the current supplier to make improvements. Often a window of time, for example, three months, may be set to allow the supplier to perform more in line with the customer's wishes. On the other hand, if the results are viewed positively, the customer is likely to renew their commitment to the choice made and be open to expanding the business with the supplier for the existing offering and other offerings that promise additional results. From this point, the process starts anew, going back to Step 1, clarifying issues, and so on.

Figure 4.3 shows the supplier steps needed to best align with the customer steps, and thus the supplier becomes more ETDBW (easy to do business with).

Figure 4.3 Aligning the Supplier Business Development Process to the Customer's Decision-Making Process

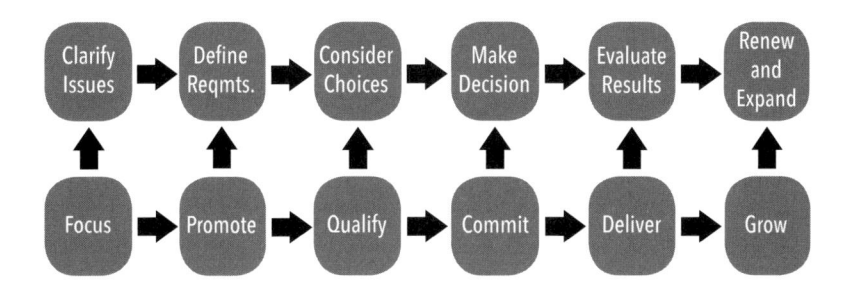

Clarify Issues → Define Reqmts. → Consider Choices → Make Decision → Evaluate Results → Renew and Expand

↑ ↑ ↑ ↑ ↑ ↑

Focus → Promote → Qualify → Commit → Deliver → Grow

Customer Success Marketing Performance System

Your marketers perform two important roles:
1. Strategic marketing, which helps build and fuel your company's strategic direction and the blueprint to implement the strategy, and
2. Tactical marketing, which supports your frontline personnel with the proper tools.

Strategic Marketing Expectations
- Build brand awareness as an industry thought leader.
- Create brand preference over competitors.

Prime activities to meet strategic marketing expectations include:
- Researching and analyzing your business environment to define and articulate your business strategy in line with customer issues and needs, your executives' leadership vision, your internal business capabilities, and your competitive position.
- Defining your customer segments based upon markets, industries, geographies, customer size, business fit, and customer philosophy toward suppliers.
- Understanding trends, issues, and what customer success looks like for your key players in your targeted prospects.
- Providing customer, market, industry, and competitor inputs to product and service development.
- Clearly understanding, creating, and communicating the appropriate value proposition that resonates with your potential customer decision makers.
- Developing appropriate market messaging and the vehicles to deliver this communication.
- Collaborating with customers and key industry players through face-to-face and online forums.
- Providing thought leadership through original research, white papers, and presentations.

Tactical Marketing Expectations

Figure 4.4 shows the two important expectations to be accomplished by marketing:

1. Turning leads — target accounts defined by the organization blueprint that fit the general profile of what the supplier customer should look like — into "suspects" — a lead that has contacted the supplier and shown interest in its capabilities.
2. Hopefully, many of these suspects have been prequalified and, thus, are already prospects when sales first touches the potential customer.

Figure 4.4 Marketing Expectations

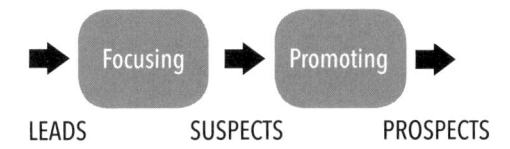

LEADS → Focusing → SUSPECTS → Promoting → PROSPECTS

Prime activities to meet tactical marketing expectations include:
- Creating and providing online tools that allow customers to qualify/disqualify themselves.
- Creating and providing tools for your sellers and servicers.
- Enticing leads and suspects to contact your organization.

Indicators of robust, quality marketing performance include:
- Your organization has strong brand awareness and brand quality.
- Your sellers have large numbers of quality prospects and high-potential suspects.

What's different about brilliant customer success marketing?
- It takes a deeper dive, with more robust research by segment and by domain.

- It strives for thought leadership. Significant effort is placed in becoming the go-to folks for trends and issues…what works and what doesn't.
- It tones down the toot. Effort is placed on not overstating claims and being more transparent about weaknesses so as to avoid customer rage at being misled.

Customer Success Selling Performance System

A robust, high-quality selling performance system supports the seller in presenting the right offerings to the right prospects at the right time in the right way.

Seller Expectations
Figure 4.5 shows the two primary expectations of sales:
1. Turning suspects into prospects.
2. Turning prospects — organizations that have a fair probability of being sold and gaining value from the sale — into customers — a prospect that buys from a supplier for the first time.

Figure 4.5 Selling Expectations

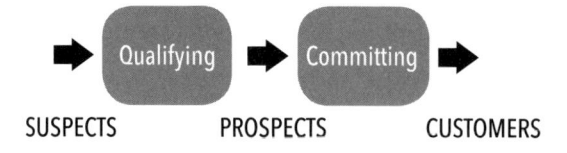

SUSPECTS → Qualifying → PROSPECTS → Committing → CUSTOMERS

Prime activities to meet selling expectations include:
- Disqualifying probable "bad" business.
- Qualifying potential good business.
- For must-have accounts, researching the prospect's past history, current situation, issues, needs, wants, and expectations in order to tailor the selling message.
- Candidly challenging customers to think differently.

- Crafting appropriate, high-impact recommendations.
- Inviting services personnel into the selling process to make sure that the customer promise can be delivered upon as well as to build trust with the prospect.
- Persuading prospects to commit to actions that will drive customer success.

What's different about brilliant customer success selling?
- It takes a deeper dive, with more robust research for must-have accounts.
- It focuses on acting as advisor. Significant effort is placed on becoming the go-to folks for trends and issues, what works and what doesn't.
- It backs off the "brag." Effort is placed on being more transparent and realistic about claims and what the customer will get and will not get.
- Traditional qualification is based primarily on determining the likelihood of the prospect buying. That is still a consideration in customer success selling, however, the likelihood of the prospect staying a customer is a more important consideration.

An indicator of robust, quality sales performance includes:
- Your sellers close 75% or more of qualified prospects.

Figure 4.6 displays the two expectations of services:
1. Turning customers into clients—customers that buy again and again.
2. Turning clients into champions—emotionally loyal clients that go out of their way to sing the praises of the supplier.

In most organizations, because of the frequency of contact, people in a service role have the biggest impact on customer experience, success, and loyalty. Think about yourself: If you bought

Figure 4.6 Services Expectations

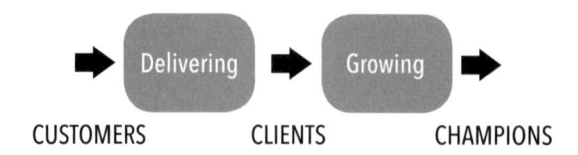

→ Delivering → Growing →
CUSTOMERS   CLIENTS   CHAMPIONS

a new car and choose to have it serviced at the dealership, your long-term perspective of the quality of the dealer is greatly biased by your perception of the service manager and the service tech, not the sales guy you never see again. Hence, robust service quality is paramount to making the brilliant customer success performance chain work. Prime activities to meet servicing expectations include:
1. Setting (sometimes re-setting) and managing realistic expectations.
2. Doing work on time, within budget, and up to quality standards.
3. Making it easy for the customer to work with your company.
4. Gaining trust and building relationships.
5. Initiating service recovery efforts when things go south.
6. Increasing customer success by influencing the customer to do the right thing.

What's different about brilliant customer success servicing?
- It is much more proactive and strategic in making recommendations.
- Service technicians act as customer advisors—assuming a more consultative role.
- It is more commercial, with more focus on customer acumen.
- Service and support personnel take an active role in pre-sales.

Indicators of robust, quality services performance include:
- The percentage of your key customers that are clients.

- The percentage of clients that are champions.

Study Findings Related to Performance Systems
- Some participants stated that necessary metrics were not defined.
- Cross-functional alignment was mentioned as a challenge.
- Issues were brought up indicating that the appropriate processes were lacking.

Performance System Recommendations
- Start with determining the customer decision-making process and what the supplier can do to best support it, and then build internal processes and actions to align and enable it.
- Clearly define who owns processes and tasks within each process step.
- Develop goals and the metrics that measure them across functions at both a team and an individual level.
- Tout your value, but be appropriately transparent about shortcomings — customers never forget if they feel they were misled.
- Make sure team members understand the goals and incentives so they align and support, and not divide and compete.
- Start with a performance system assessment to compare where you are to where you need to go.

Figure 4.7 shows the high-level elements of a customer success performance system assessment. Each of the five capabilities of your frontline team and the six performance levers need to be explored. I also recommend that at the same time you investigate the quality and appropriateness of your process for recruiting, hiring, developing, and retaining your top talent. Many more performance system-related recommendations integrated into touchpoint management recommendations will be discussed shortly.

Figure 4.7 Customer Success Performance System Assessment

OBJECTIVES
- Assess the current talent effectiveness of the customer success team.
- Discover gaps and make recommendations for improvements in performance.

FOCUS - **15 Success Factors**

Performance Levers	Capabilities	Talent Process
1. Expectations	7. Relationship Skills	12. Recruiting
2. Tools	8. Proactive Mindset	13. Hiring
3. Metrics	9. Customer Acumen	14. Developing
4. Consequences	10. Engagement Management	15. Retaining
5. Feedback	11. Technical Proficiency	
6. Processes		

POSSIBLE METHODS
- Review of all relevant documents.
- Personal interviews with senior executives and select managers.
- Focus group of star frontline people and focus group of average-performing frontline people
- Surveys.
- In-the-field observation.

Enabling Technology

Traditional Technology

In the old days, technology management was always expensive, usually slow, and mostly focused on the past. Mention the name of your ERP or CRM and most people cringe. People did the best they could with reports not ideal to their situation and cobbled together data from disparate systems in Excel to try and make sense out of it.

For the challenges of delivering customer success, this approach is lousy.

An enabling technology is required to make sure the right people have the right information at the right time.[2] This has been an organizational challenge for over a century, but new customer success tools such as live experience tracking (LET) allow the capture of key online and offline information that bring home the moments of truth in real time.

Study Findings Related to Enabling Technology
- A high percentage of study participants had issues concerning the quality of the information they had, compared to what they felt they needed.
- There was general recognition that customer success technology is a valuable asset to all organizations wanting to deliver customer success.
- Study participants felt that customer success management technologies pay off handsomely.
- Many stated that their organizations needed new technology to better support their customer success efforts.

Enabling Technology Recommendations
- Appropriate technologies power all performance systems — don't scrimp on technology investments; buying the very best available is a wise decision.
- Proactively address issues before they turn into problems by using the predictive analytics available in customer success technologies.[3]
- Use your technology to develop a "health score dashboard"[4] to help your customer success team monitor and adjust based upon the metrics most important to your business. For example, your health score might combine elements such as activity level, feature adoption, support history, loyalty scores, and relationship strength.

Chapter Summary

To be successful, even the most brilliant racecar driver needs talented mechanics and a top-notch pit crew to win. The same is true of your frontline customer success team. Give them the guidance, tools, and feedback so that they can win with the customer, and then add in the appropriate technology to speed and smooth the process.

CHAPTER 5

Touchpoint Management

Chapter 2 outlined my recommended approach to kick-starting an emphasis on the customer experience by using the Hassle Meter to gain interest and start the touchpoint management process. This chapter goes into more specific detail on how to put touchpoint management to work in your organization.

Any contact the customer has with your organization will have an impact on their experience. Once the customer has decided to engage with your organization at some level, the vast majority of the impact will come from frontline personnel contact either face-to-face, via telephone, or online. However, usually the customer is touched by the supplier organization much further upstream in other less-personal ways, such as advertisements, Google searches, your website, downloaded brochures, videos, and so forth. Often these early customer experiences greatly impact the customer's decision to desire more personal supplier contact.

For the supplier wanting to create customer success while delivering brilliant customer experiences, the first question to ask, and then answer, is: What does the customer want, expect, and deserve during each of those six customer decision-making steps? Our guide will be the seven things customers want, expect, and deserve, introduced in Chapter 2.

Figure 5.1 builds off of my earlier discussion on aligning supplier steps with customer steps and completes the touchpoint management model by adding more components. When the supplier performs brilliantly while providing the appropriate credible, relevant, usable information needed at each decision-making step, customers are motivated to continue the supplier relationship and move on together to the next step. I will take you through these steps one by one.

Figure 5.1 Touchpoint Management

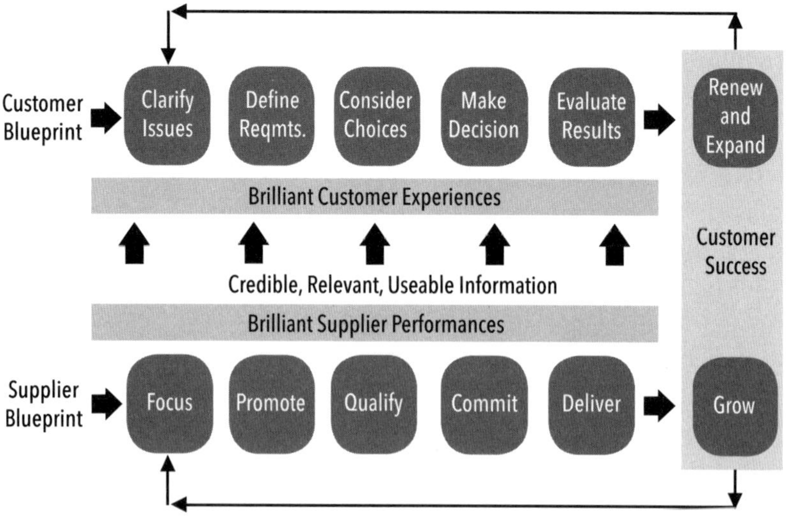

Cruising Vacation Example

To make this section clearer, more interesting, and hopefully more fun, I will share an imaginary family example that we can all relate to in order to illustrate how touchpoint mapping works. After each supplier step, I will describe the customer and supplier actions in the Cruising Vacation example. Here is the background.

The Prospective Customer
The Graswalds are a middle-class family (Mark the dad, Helen the mom, Dusty the son, and Aubrey the daughter) who are exploring options for their annual vacation. In the past, their family vacations have been an adventure in Las Vegas, an exciting trip to Europe, and a fascinating family gathering over Christmas. This year they decide that if they can afford it, they would like to take a cruise over Thanksgiving break.

The Supplier
The North American division of Festival Cruise Lines is the supplier. Their target market segment is middle-class families.

Step One: Aligning Supplier Focus to Help the Customer Clarify Issues

As discussed earlier, focusing defines the playing field of the supplier by:
- Determining customer segments based upon markets, industries, geographies, customer size, business fit, and customer philosophy toward suppliers.
- Articulating, in detail, market issues and trends, and customer issues and trends, by segment.
- Providing customer, market, industry, and competitor inputs to product and service development.

- Developing the value propositions of supplier offerings by segment.
- Identifying and targeting the executives of potential customers, as they are individuals tasked with addressing their critical business issues.

If the potential customers in your defined segments are not aware of you and your offerings, or they don't like your message, the customer experience ends with you never being made aware of the possible sale—just like when you were a youngster and the boy or girl of your dreams lived next door but you never met... how sad.

However, if your message gets through and resonates with the potential customer, your focusing efforts will help the customer clarify issues and define requirements. Thus, the customer may invite you to be considered as an option as the they evaluate alternatives.

For the step of focusing, the supplier marketing group needs to ask, answer, and then address three questions:

1. What does the customer need to help them clarify issues?
   A. Credible, relevant, usable information to gain a good understanding of critical trends, problems, and opportunities their industry faces.
   B. Brilliant customer experiences with every supplier interaction.

2. What does the supplier want from the step of focusing?
   A. Demonstrate thought leadership.
   B. Showcase expertise.
   C. Develop market awareness and credibility.

3. How should the supplier respond?
   A. Use its deep and wide understanding of the targeted

market to educate potential customers on critical issues, their importance, and the possible implications of various actions.
B. Perform brilliantly at each customer touchpoint.

Possible Performance Tools
Research studies, white papers, books, articles, and case studies are all possible tools to convey the credible, relevant, usable information the customer needs.

Possible Vehicles
These performance tools can be delivered in a variety of ways to best suit the preferences of the customer. Your marketing vehicles might be:
- Traditional advertising.
- Joining or sponsoring executive events at conferences or independently.
- Giving speeches at executive forums or industry conferences.
- Conducting webcasts.
- Writing articles, white papers, or books.
- Promotional literature.
- Word of mouth and word of mouse.
- Downloads from websites.
- Electronic newsletters.
- YouTube videos.
- Press releases.
- Giving interviews.
- A supplier booth at trade shows.

Possible Performance Metrics

- Quantity: Percentage of potential customers in a defined segment who know who you are.
- Quality: Percentage of potential customers in a defined seg-

ment who know who you are and have a positive perception of you.
- Cost: Cost of focusing (all costs associated with developing and implementing the tools and vehicles described above).
- Time: Cycle time of focusing, e.g., once a campaign is started, the length of time it takes to reach a certain level of awareness or recognition.

If the customer is satisfied with the supplier information provided and the supplier performance, there is a high probability that the customer will engage the supplier in their next decision step.

Graswald Decision-Making Process Step One: Clarifying Issues

The executive team (Mark and Helen) define their most important issues as "everyone has fun on the cruise with no hassles." Pretty basic, but clear.

Festival Step One: Focusing to Help the Customer Clarify Issues

Their extensive market research has identified the main issues, wants, and needs of this category, and the Festival value proposition is Good-Value Family Fun. For years Festival has routinely placed ads during the TV shows that middle-class moms, dads, and kids watch and in the magazines they read. All of their advertisements picture smiling families on board one of their ships with blue skies above and bluer water below. Their marketing folks have spent much time and money on building the brand. Obviously it has paid off, as Mark and Helen have heard of Festival Cruise Lines and their biggest competitor, Endless Summer Cruise Lines, and have a neutral to positive impression of both.

Commentary: Off to a good start. As the marketers reading this know well, branding is a long-term endeavor.

Step Two: Aligning Supplier Promoting to Help the Customer Define Requirements

While focusing is strategic, promoting is all about tactics—clear messaging that creates awareness, shows expertise, presents a value proposition, and generates interest.

For the step of promoting, the supplier needs to ask, answer, and then address three questions:

1. What does the customer need to define requirements?
    A. Credible, relevant, usable information to gain a good understanding of what is needed in a solution to their issue.
    B. Brilliant customer experiences with every supplier interaction.

2. What does the supplier want?
    A. Build its brand as a credible supplier of appropriate solutions.
    B. Influence the customer to accept its definition of a solution.
    C. Persuade the customer that its solution is a good option.
    D. Get the customer to engage with the supplier.

3. How should the supplier respond?
    A. Use its deep and wide understanding of the critical issues of the targeted market and various offerings to help potential customers establish the criteria of an appropriate solution.
    B. Perform brilliantly at each customer touchpoint.

Possible Performance Tools
Along with the same tools suggested during focusing, case stud-

ies can be an excellent tool, as they demonstrate how other customers facing similar issues defined their requirements appropriately. Brochures can also highlight the key points you want to emphasize.

Possible Vehicles
The same vehicles used in focusing are also good choices for promoting. In addition, your people and/or channel partners may also serve as touchpoint vehicles via chat or email, by phone, or in person. In many cases, live or web-based demonstrations are often good methods.

Possible Performance Metrics

1. Quantity:
   - Percentage of potential customers in a defined segment who associate you with your market message and value proposition.
   - Number of potential customers that engage with the supplier.
2. Quality: Percentage of potential customers in a defined segment who associate you with your market message and value proposition and have a positive perception of you.
3. Cost: Cost of promoting.
4. Time: Cycle time of promoting.

If the customer is engaged and positive about the supplier experience, the customer will want the supplier to help them with the next step.

Graswald Decision-Making Process Step Two: Defining Requirements
After several sit-downs at the family dinner table, the requirements established for the cruise where:

1. Must not exceed the budget. (Mark is already stretching things).
2. All-inclusive meals. (Dusty eats like a thrasher.)
3. Destination is the Caribbean. (Helen has always dreamed of going to this romantic locale.)
4. Ship must have at least two swimming pools. (Both kids love the water.)
5. Lots of organized activities for the kids. (Aubrey is a demanding princess and Mom and Dad want some time alone.)

Festival Step Two: Promoting to Help in Defining Requirements

Along with everything Festival is doing, as mentioned in Step One, they have a strong online presence. In addition to creating awareness and building a positive presence, they try to set the stage for what makes up a good family cruise. They have their own *Savvy Cruiser* blog with posts such as "The 10 Must-Haves of Family Cruises," "Cruises that Won't Bust Your Budget," "Let the Staff Babysit the Kids," and so on.

Commentary: Sounds like Festival is in line with the Graswald's thinking and may be able to shape those requirements in their favor.

Step Three: Aligning Supplier Qualifying to Help the Customer Consider Choices

If the potential customer engaged with you during the past step, they may have accepted all or part of the criteria you suggested. This is good for the supplier, as it improves the supplier position. If the potential customer did not engage with you this may not be good news, as they may have been influenced by a competitor that sees the world differently. Either way, you again start this step with considering what the potential customer needs.

For the step of qualifying, the supplier needs to ask, answer, and then address three questions:

1. What does the customer need to help them consider choices effectively?
   A. Credible, relevant, usable information to easily eliminate those solutions that do not meet the criteria established during the defining requirements stage and to objectively compare and contrast different options that do meet the criteria to come up with a shortlist of possible solutions/suppliers.
   B. Brilliant customer experiences with every supplier interaction.

2. What does the supplier want?
   A. To quickly disqualify probable bad customers.
   B. To quickly qualify potential customers that have the probability to become good customers.
   C. To gain a position on the potential good customer's shortlist of suppliers.

3. How should the supplier respond?
   A. Use its deep and wide understanding of past and current customers to establish the characteristics of good (and bad) customers to develop a qualifying checklist.
   B. Gather specific information about each prospective customer relevant to the qualifying checklist.
   C. Reactively encourage prospective customers to qualify or disqualify themselves by making a self-qualifying tool easily accessible.
   D. Proactively and personally engage high-potential customers to qualify them.
   E. Perform brilliantly at each customer touchpoint.

Possible Performance Tools

Along with the same outputs generated during the steps of focusing and promoting, a qualifying checklist that describes the characteristics of a good customer need and supplier fit is essential. Ideally, a qualifying tool is available online so that potential customers can disqualify or qualify the supplier's solution. In addition, a qualifying checklist should be put in the hands of frontline personnel trained in the qualifying process. Sample cases of both good and bad qualifiers can be powerful examples. Simple assessments can be used to make the customer aware of your criteria and get them to interact with various choices and possible effects. Financial calculators can add credibility. Figure 5.2 shares a tool to help you quantify and qualify.

Figure 5.2 The Qualifying Checklist

SUSPECTS → Qualifying → PROSPECTS

SUCCESS FACTORS	Low High
1. Importance to the account	1 2 3 4 5 6 7 8 9 10
2. Business fit	1 2 3 4 5 6 7 8 9 10
3. Personal fit	1 2 3 4 5 6 7 8 9 10
4. Our reputation with the account	1 2 3 4 5 6 7 8 9 10
5. Account partnership attitude	1 2 3 4 5 6 7 8 9 10
6. Competitive position	1 2 3 4 5 6 7 8 9 10
7. Access to decision makers	1 2 3 4 5 6 7 8 9 10
8. Funding	1 2 3 4 5 6 7 8 9 10
9. Importance to us	1 2 3 4 5 6 7 8 9 10
10. Timing	1 2 3 4 5 6 7 8 9 10

Source: Adapted from *The Knowledge-Based Organization*. James Alexander and Michael Lyons. Irwin. 1995.

Here are the steps required for you to develop and use your own qualifying checklist. Invest a few hours and involve a few key folks, say a team of five to seven, including those responsible for selling, consulting, and finance, to:

1. Analyze the last five or six "good" sales your company made (fast sells with good profit margins and happy clients), and talk about why these were successful. Look for root causes. Next, think of and talk through the last few big non-sales (lots of time and money spent, but no business), and discuss why these efforts were unsuccessful. It takes a little digging, but some common elements will be revealed.
2. Use the above information to determine the 5 to 10 success factors that are most important to your organization in procuring good business. Clearly define each factor and write down examples (you will have to communicate this to the rest of the organization later). Make sure that there is agreement on meanings and consensus on the factors selected. Finally, put your factors into a checklist format that allows quantification.
3. Test your checklist by scoring a few of the past sales and non-sales discussed in Step 1. You will find a big difference in the scores of these two groups. Modify your factors and the definitions until you are satisfied with their appropriateness.
4. Apply the checklist to your current prospects. This will open some eyes. Ask the people on your team who are involved in selling to take five minutes (that's all it takes) to score two or three of their current prospects. It is not uncommon for the team to realize that 25 percent or more of the prospects being pursued are bad prospects—virtually a zero chance of procuring profitable business.
5. Systematize use of the checklist. In two-hour to four-hour sessions, introduce it to all your people involved in selling. Explain its use and have everyone use the checklist to qualify existing prospects. This is a great way to help the selling team discover what quality selling is all about and to help them focus resources on the best bets. It also will make you cognizant of the reality of your existing forecast.
6. Use the checklist as a management tool. At this point, every-

one in the organization has a common vocabulary. Use the key success factors as a feedback guide to understand and manage selling resources. The more you use it, the better you will become at forecasting and filling your sales funnel with high-potential business.

That's all there is to it. Invest a little time, follow the above steps, and I'd be very surprised if you don't see immediate improvements in your selling performance.

Possible Vehicles
The same vehicles used in the steps of focusing and promoting are also good choices for qualifying. For most high-potential, business-to-business, prospective customers, the qualification will involve frontline personnel trained in what good business looks like and armed with qualifying tools. They should start with an assessment to validate or invalidate the customer's assumption of requirements and conduct a reality check outlining: (1) if success is possible, and (2) what realistic efforts it will take by both the customer and the supplier to deliver on the promise. In some situations, a manager may act as quality control by reviewing each proposed qualified prospect.

Possible Performance Metrics

1. Quantity: Number of potential customers that meet your qualification criteria.
2. Quality:
   - Percentage of qualified potential customers that have a positive perception of the supplier.
   - Percentage of qualified potential customers that become customers.
3. Cost: Cost of qualifying.
4. Time: Cycle time of qualifying.

If both the prospective customer and the supplier doing the qualifying agree there is the potential for a good business fit, the process moves to the next step.

Graswald Decision-Making Process Step Three: Considering Choices
Mom goes online and searches "cruises for families with challenging children." Dad goes online and searches "cruising on the cheap." They both find several travel websites, e-magazines, and posts and start considering possibilities. They kept reading nice things about cruises, in general, which reinforced their decision to cruise. Wally World Orange Line sounded appealing until Dad eliminated them because of high cost. Festival and Endless Summer appeared the most often in their searches, and those two companies quickly became the Graswald's shortlist.

Festival Step Three: Qualifying to Help in Considering Choices
Festival touts the positive reviews of past passengers, and they host their own passenger chat room and monitor others.

From their extensive research on buying behavior, Festival knows that pricing is a big deal to many middle-income families. They had done a lot of price comparison with their competition as well as invested in "threshold pricing" that defines a range of prices that Festival would accept to get the business. When Dad typed in "five-day Caribbean cruises for under $X" in his browser, the amount he put in was actually lower than Festival's standard pricing. However, since the amount was within the pricing threshold already established by Festival, a flash reply immediately went to Dad giving their normal price, but saying that was a limited-time special offer that was a little under what he put in. Dad smiled and was leaning more and more toward Festival as the cruise line of choice.

Commentary: Smart move...by planning and predicting, Festival was able to keep a prospect who might have otherwise defected.

Step Four: Committing the Customer to Make a Decision

With the potential customer narrowing down his choices to just a few possible options, it is time for him to make a decision. Not only must the supplier convince the prospective customer that their solution is the most appropriate, they must convince him that buying and implementing the solution is worth the effort, and better than doing nothing.

For the step of committing, the supplier needs to ask, answer, and then address three questions:

1. What does the customer need to make a decision?
   A. Credible, relevant, usable information to help them make the best decision and feel confident and comfortable that their choice is worth the investment.
   B. Brilliant customer experiences with every supplier interaction.

2. What does the supplier want?
   A. Get good business.
   B. Prepare the customer for a positive delivery of the solution.
   C. Set the stage for more good business in the future.

3. How should the supplier respond?
   A. Use its deep and wide understanding of past and current customers to develop brilliant buying propositions and proposals.
   B. Using a customer success assessment as a guide (Figure 5.3), transparently engage with the customer to discuss probable and possible challenges and jointly agree on how they will be handled.
   C. Make it easy to buy.
   D. Perform brilliantly at each customer touchpoint.

Figure 5.3 Customer Success Analysis

			CUSTOMER SUCCESS	
KEY PLAYERS	**TITLE**	**ROLE**	**BUSINESS OUTCOMES**	**PERSONAL WINS**
Phillip Thomas	CIO	D	Maximize uptime. Demonstrate financial impact.	Peer recognition as innovator. Minimal hassle.
Suzanne Bio	IT Mgr.	I	System failures. Minimize downtime.	Waiting for retirement. Don't rock the boat.
Bubba Gomez	Netw. Admin.	U	Minimize downtime. Loves cool technology.	Wants to be promoted. Likes to be in control.

Roles: Deciders   Approvers   Influencers   Users   Coaches

Possible Performance Tools

Along with the same tools generated during focusing, promoting, and qualifying, testimonials can be an especially powerful influencing tool at this stage. Outside expert research (e.g., consumer reports, Gartner Magic Quadrant, and so on) can add impact. A customer success assessment is a great input to the implementation plan. In addition, a financial analysis developed with potential customer input can often help the customer justify the decision to themselves and others in their organization.

For complex situations, key events may need to be committed to (e.g., product demonstrations, test customer visits, trial pilots, assessments) and successfully implemented before the big sale is made. Depending upon the complexity of the situation, a formal readiness assessment checklist can help both the supplier and the customer plot their onboarding strategy.

Possible Vehicles

The same vehicles used in focusing, promoting, and qualifying are used in this step. Short YouTube videos can add impact. For important customers, personal touch is required: guiding prospects to positive comments either by word of mouth or word of mouse, encouraging prospects to visit forums that discuss supplier products, taking customers on visits to supplier headquarters, or better yet, visits with satisfied customers.

Possible Performance Metrics

1. Quantity:
   - Number of new customers.
   - Free trial conversion rate.
2. Quality:
   - Win ratio (percentage of proposals that close).
   - Customer perception.
3. Cost: Cost of sale.
4. Time: Cycle time of selling.

If the prospective customer becomes a customer, the process moves on to the next step.

Graswald Decision-Making Process Step Four: Making a Decision

Once their friend, Carmela, said she loved the cruise she took with her kids on Festival, Mom and Dad were almost ready to go with Festival. Dad, however, said that they should also take a closer look at Endless Summer Cruise Line just to compare. Sitting side by side they decided to call each cruise line to answer their questions. They first called Festival and were immediately connected to a real live person. They were impressed that there was no waiting and no phone tree asking them to "press 1" for this and "press 2" for that. The agent was pleasant, thoughtful, knowledgeable, and quite helpful. She questioned them on must-haves and wants, she gave them choices of dates and ships and destinations. She sounded very positive about Festival and confident that they would just love sailing. After hearing them out, she recommended sailing on the Enchantress for the five-day Northern Carribbean cruise departing from Miami on November 25.

Mom and Dad looked at each other, smiled, nodded, and the deal was done. Credit card out, down payment made, and Endless Summer, cluelessly, was eliminated from a contest they never knew they were in.

Festival Step Four: Committing to Help the Customer in Making a Decision
Festival knows the power of word of mouth and has spent a lot of time developing their Frequent Floater Awards system that offers many perks for influencing others to take their first cruise with them. Maybe their friend, Carmela, was especially enthusiastic in recommending Festival because that referral entitled her family to a free excursion on their next cruise. ;)

Festival also knows that personal touch is a powerful persuasion tool. They spend significant time and money on hiring for attitude and smarts, training on relationship-building and influencing skills, coaching on those behaviors, and rewarding based on customer feedback and closing business. They arm their agents with a host of tools. Based upon their investment in talent, they know that once someone calls Festival, there is a high probability that the prospect will commit before the call is completed.

Commentary: These Festival folks seem to have the first four steps down pat.

Step Five: Delivering on the Promise to Help the Customer Evaluate Results

Depending upon the solution purchased, the supplier time and effort required to implement a solution may range from a few keystrokes taking minutes for a cloud-based offering, to years of heavy lifting for a hardware and software installation of a traditional ERP. Implementing a solution on time and up to quality is, of course, important, however, there is much more that needs to be done for the delivering step to be successful. Delivering on the promise means accomplishing the mutually agreed-upon desired outcome (customer success) and doing so within the time taken to achieve that outcome (time to value).

Delivering is a process unto itself consisting of multiple steps sometimes occurring in order, but often occurring simultaneously, as shown in Figure 5.4.

Figure 5.4 Delivering on the Promise

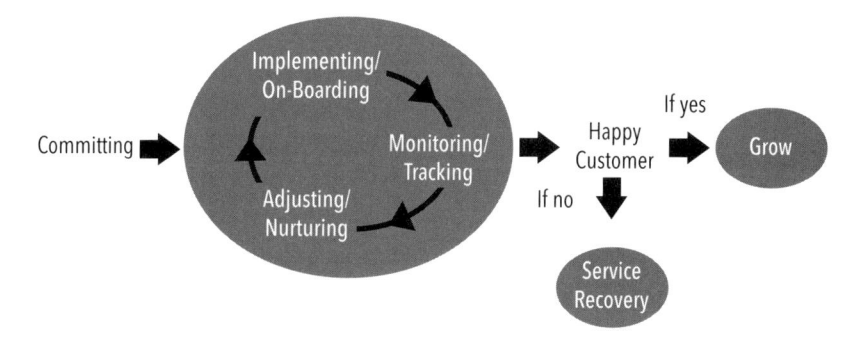

1. Implementing and On-Boarding

At no time in the supplier-customer relationship is the customer more excited and motivated to learn and invest time to receive the benefits of the promise they have bought than directly after committing to a solution. On-boarding (e.g., immediate training, easy access to information, and personal follow-up of select users) should start on day one, hour one, of implementation to help keep the momentum going.

2. Adjusting and Nurturing

Even the most thoughtful plan will need to be changed. Hence, actions need to be modified to adjust to new realities that will naturally occur. Nurturing is required to keep key customer personnel feeling positive, and keep things moving forward.

3. Monitoring and Tracking

Usage and performance monitoring also starts immediately and continues throughout delivery and beyond. Ongoing reports to the customer and to the team demonstrate progress (usage and/or results), discuss problems and their status, and predict issues that will probably occur in the future. When Step 2, Adjusting and Nurturing, is not successful, service recovery is called for with red lights flashing and sirens blaring to quickly address any issues before they get out of control.

For the step of delivering, the supplier needs to ask, answer, and then address three questions:

1. What does the customer need?
    A. Credible, relevant, usable information to help them evaluate the results of what they bought.
    B. Training and coaching to encourage usage.
    C. Ongoing feedback that demonstrates they have made the right decision.
    D. Immediate service recovery if issues occur.
    E. Brilliant customer experiences with every supplier interaction.

2. What does the supplier want?
    A. To efficiently and effectively implement the solution to deliver on the promise.
    B. To build the base for growth.
    C. To set the stage for a powerful testimonial.

3. How should the supplier respond?
    A. Use its deep and wide understanding of past and current

customer delivery plus information gathered about the uniqueness of the customer to do it right the first time.
B. Transparently discuss with the customer probable and possible challenges to delivery, and jointly agree on how they will be handled.
C. Communicate regularly on delivery status.
D. Do it very right the second time (service recovery) when significant issues arise.
E. Perform brilliantly at each customer touchpoint.

Possible Performance Tools
Along with the same outputs generated during the steps of focusing, promoting, qualifying, and committing, delivery updates communicating project status are a valuable tool that can minimize customer anxiety and quickly uncover any issues needing action. Agreed-upon service recovery and escalation processes can speed and smooth issue resolution. Enabling technologies allow for real-time proactive monitoring.

Possible Vehicles
The same vehicles used in the steps of focusing, promoting, qualifying, and committing are used in this step. For important customers, high levels of personal touch may be required, e.g., monitoring/coaching key players and face-to-face quarterly reviews.

Possible Performance Metrics

1. Quantity: Number of defectors/adopters.
2. Quality: Customer perception.
3. Cost: Cost of delivering.
4. Time:
    - Time to implementation completion.
    - Time to value.

If the customer is satisfied with delivery, the process moves on to the next step.

Graswald Decision-Making Process Step Five: Evaluating Results

As promised, within 15 minutes of committing to the cruise the Graswalds received their booking confirmation that was accurate and clear. They also received weekly emails with travel tips and more details on the ship's entertainment and other "for a small price" options. In fact, they were so enticed that they signed up, and paid up front, for an Aruba Sunset Cruise and a four-wheeler jungle excursion in Puerto Rico. Everyone in the family was excited...they envisioned the perfect experience with every moment being wonderful. They told everyone they met about the cruise and what a wonderful experience it would be.

However, no one told them that they would have to stand in line two hours and 35 minutes (most of it in the hot Miami sun) to go through security, the "initial" passenger sign-up, and two more stops that made no sense to any of the line-standers. The kids were complaining and wandering off, Dad was getting angrier by the moment, and Mom had the harried look of someone who might lose it.

The ship signage was confusing and their map was difficult to interpret, so it took them close to an hour to find their cabin amidst the traffic of 4,000-plus other passengers. When their cabin door closed, they were tired and hungry. By the time they had settled in, they had missed the welcome lunch and had to wait two and a half hours for the dinner lines to open. Although Mom and Dad said they would allow themselves one cocktail per day, Mom found her way to the Lido deck while Dad was in the bathroom and had chucked down two margaritas and a pinot grigio before Dad tracked her down. As Dad ordered a beer, he looked at the drink prices and started to question whether this cruise was the right decision.

Festival Step Five: Delivering on the Promise
Festival committed a cardinal sin: not being transparent. They knew quite well that their process of getting people onto the ship was not good…they knew of the long lines in the heat and humidity, but they chose not to inform their guests.

This dark cloud of the initial ship experience lightened over the course of many fun experiences, but it never went away. The sense of betrayal from being deliberately misled was always in the back of the Graswald's minds.

Even though they told all their family and friends they had a great time, Mom and Dad agreed they would consider another cruise sometime, but they questioned whether they would ever do a "big ship" cruise again, and they both agreed that traveling with Festival a second time was highly unlikely.

By the way, they never complained, as they thought it would do no good and just be a waste of time.

Commentary: The "on-boarding" experience was not good.

Step Six: Growing the Account to Help Renew and Expand

For the step of growing, the supplier needs to ask, answer, and then address three questions:

1. What does the customer need to renew and expand?
    A. Credible, relevant, usable information to help them receive and communicate the success they have achieved and feel the desire to use more of the supplier's offerings.
    B. Brilliant customer experiences with every supplier interaction.

2. What does the supplier want?
    A. Efficient and effective performance.
    B. Renewal of initial business.

C. Expansion of new business.
   D. Customers who are supplier champions.

3. How should the supplier respond?
   A. Use its deep and wide understanding of the customer to commit the customer to more business.
   B. Communicate transparently and regularly on performance status and ideas to make the customer even more successful.
   C. Perform brilliantly at each customer touchpoint.

Possible Performance Tools
Along with the same tools generated during focusing, promoting, qualifying, committing, and delivering, customer-specific assessments, reports, and recommendations should be developed to uncover opportunities and plan action. Comparisons against industry standards or direct competitors can be powerful tools to take action.

Possible Vehicles
The same vehicles used in focusing, promoting, qualifying, committing, and delivering are used in this step. A process of regular customer/supplier reviews (e.g., quarterly business reviews) can be a powerful way to demonstrate supplier commitment, showcase performance, discover opportunities, and build relationships.

Possible Performance Metrics

1. Quantity:
   - Percentage of customers that renew or those that don't (churn rate).
   - Amount of new sales by customer.
   - Monthly reoccurring revenue.

2. Quality: Percentage of customers that recommend the supplier.
3. Cost: Cost of growing.
4. Time: Time to next purchase commitment.

As new growth opportunities are jointly explored, the process returns to the supplier helping the customer to clarify issues, define requirements, and so on.

Graswald Step Six: Renewing and Expanding
The Graswalds never took another Festival cruise, however, three years later they did do another family cruise with Endless Summer Cruise Lines with some friends.

Festival Step Six: Growing the Account to Help Renew and Expand
Before they left the ship, Festival plied the Graswald's with special deals on upcoming cruises. They sent out an extensive feedback form and did weekly e-mailings until the Graswald's unsubscribed. A personal phone call might have let Festival know how they really felt and given them a chance for service recovery.

Commentary: Although they performed brilliantly in most moments of truth, this family case study shows how just one weak link in the customer success chain cost Festival dearly. Consider lost lifetime value — it is not uncommon for "frequent floaters" to take two or three cruises per year for many years....and, the kids will grow up some day and have money to take cruises on their own. All this is lost opportunity.

Touchpoint Management Study Findings

- Basically, the touchpoint requirements of delivering customer success are the same for both traditional and subscription organizations.

- Switching costs are almost always much higher for the customers of on-premise suppliers.
- However...in the subscription model, there is a need for speed—because of much lower switching costs, very active involvement of customer-facing personnel in the first days directly after the purchase is a requirement to minimize churn.
- Customer success management should be viewed from an organizational, team, and individual level with cascading goals and the metrics to measure success aligned.

Touchpoint Management Recommendations

- Use the six steps of the customer success delivery process to align your actions to what the customer needs during each of the six steps of the customer decision-making process. (Remember that customers don't always know what they need. Sometimes the customer success team has to gently but persuasively help the customer define appropriate requirements.)
- Clearly define ownership of the customer success delivery process and all tasks that comprise it.
- Actively follow the seven things that every customer wants, expects, and deserves throughout the process for every customer contact.
- Invest in market segment research that will showcase your thought leadership and highlight your capabilities.
- Translate your knowledge into the language that your marketplace understands and values.
- Make your market message compelling and clear, concise and consistent.
- Tout your value, but be appropriately transparent about shortcomings—customers never forget if they feel they were misled.

- Let your customers learn the way they want to learn—provide a variety of tools and the vehicles to deliver them.
- Use an appropriate mix of one-to-one, one-to-few, and one-to-many to deliver on the promise.
- Give the customer choices—standard, tailored, or custom offerings—and market, price, sell, and deliver accordingly.
- Conduct a customer success analysis for every prospect.
- Develop a qualifying checklist and require its use when considering any new business.
- Introduce the customer to the post-sales team before the deal is finalized.
- Allow the post-sales team to have input into proposals and to say no to bad business.
- Jointly build an adoption/on-boarding plan during the qualifying process, and start on-boarding immediately after committing.
- Create a service recovery process, and empower everyone on the team to initiate immediately, as needed.[1]
- Collaborate. When the customer participates, solutions are better, problems are preempted, and trust is built.
- Have a need for speed. Compressing the cycle time of all aspects of the customer success process is important, but the magical month (the first 30 days after customer commitment) is vital.
- Take a holistic approach. Customer success implementation impacts all people and all processes across your organization.
- For traditional organizations transitioning to customer success management, recognize and address the significant cultural change required.
- First, understand your customer decision-making process. You can then align brilliant employee performances that deliver brilliant customer experiences.
- Let touchpoint management guide your action during all moments of truth.

- Measure the metrics that matter most: retention, growth, customer loyalty, and time to value.

Chapter Summary

Touchpoint management is where the rubber meets the road. Supplier success depends upon knowing and aligning with the six customer decision-making steps and giving customers what they want, expect, and deserve at each moment of truth. Like a champion relay team, smooth handoffs drive optimum performance.

CHAPTER 6

Brilliant Leadership

No matter what type of organization you have, it is your leadership's role to craft and build the appropriate culture, and frame and implement the organizational blueprint.

Culture

In many ways this is the easiest link in the customer success performance chain to understand, yet the most difficult to forge or break. Culture is the set of shared, taken-for-granted, implicit assumptions that a group holds and that determines how it perceives and reacts to its various environments.[1] It is the primary role of the organization leader to create the culture in the start-up phase, nurture it during growth, and modify or destroy it in maturity. Culture:
- Is the result of actions over many years.
- Is the biggest source of resistance to change.

- Directly impacts an organization's long-term economic performance. The benefits can be dramatic, as high-performing cultures showed 682% growth over 11 years compared to 166% for everyone else.[2]

High-performing cultures share four components in common:[3]
- **Contribution.** Contribution refers to the actual value added by either the individual or the group or groups within which people operate. Contribution is a part of a culture when (1) results are valued more than hard work, (2) performance is more important than political connections in getting recognized and rewarded, (3) individuals are expected to take personal responsibility for their actions, and (4) there is a tolerance of unusual styles of behavior of the people who do good work.
- **Candor.** Candor is a part of a culture when (1) people are frank, even when ideas directly confront those of superiors, (2) people challenge the unsupported talk and actions of others, (3) people routinely stop to reflect about what they are doing and why, and (4) exemplary performers are regularly observed and analyzed to fuel improvement efforts.
- **Community.** Community is a spirit of interdependence among individuals within the supplier, its partners, the customer, and people within the organizations within the marketplace. The sense of community spurs the sharing of information, respect, and openness.
- **Constant learning.** Constant learning has special significance in making a culture amenable to change, because in order to constantly learn, an organization must actively listen, understand, and align with the issues and the feelings of all stakeholders. Organizations with this element built-in are open to ongoing change because they see meeting stakeholder needs as an element of the culture. Constant learning is a part of a culture when (1) continuous improvement is valued, (2) in-

novation is prized, (3) appropriate knowledge-management systems are in place, and (4) quality failure is acceptable.

Culture of Success

Even in organizations possessing high-performance cultures as described above, one more cultural dimension is needed to deliver customer success. This requires that a supplier embraces and operates based upon customer intimacy—a deep understanding of how the customer thinks and acts and what they value (Figure 6.1). Customer intimacy means that all aspects of the organization are focused on making all customers (or at least some segments) successful as each customer defines it. When customer intimacy is embedded within and throughout the organization, customer success follows. In short, this philosophy means "when the customer wins, we win."

FIGURE 6.1 Culture of Success

| Customer Intimacy | Contribution | Candor | Constant Learning | Community |

Easy to say, but sometimes very, very challenging to do—remember the earlier discussion on being customer oblivious?

Compelling Blueprint

The second prime responsibility of leadership is to craft and then oversee the implementation of the organization blueprint. Under leadership guidance, the marketing organization or the strategy group gathers, sorts, and analyzes the information required in the development of a compelling blueprint. External data gathering and analysis, including methods such as environmental scanning, voice of the customer research, brand perception/credibility analysis, and competitive positioning, are combined with internal data gathering and analysis, including the collection of perceptions and the comparison of external issues and needs to internal capabilities. These inputs help define the supplier organization's focus of ideal markets, offerings, and customers, plus a rich understanding of the issues and trends of the target market.

A compelling blueprint creates common ground, defines expectations, establishes decision-making criteria, and builds consensus and commitment. It is the high-level action plan for making customer success management a reality. A robust blueprint contains the following eight components:

1. **Mission.** What the organization does.
2. **Vision.** The preferred future of the organization.
3. **Values.** Shared beliefs and principles that serve as guidelines for behavior.
4. **Goals.** The broad targets that measure organizational success.
5. **Focus.** The organization's ideal markets, offerings, and customers.
6. **Distinct competencies.** Attributes and capabilities that provide unique benefits to customers.
7. **Critical business issues.** The most important problems or opportunities that can or will impact organization success.
8. **Organization design.** The internal structure and outside channels most appropriate to implement the blueprint.

Below are some findings from my research along with some recommendations related to leadership.

Study Findings Related to Leadership

- The proven concepts of strategic account management[4] is an appropriate framework for delivering customer success no matter what the supplier business.

- For the most part, customer success was spoken of by research participants in tactical, not strategic terms, demonstrating a disconnect between what is desired and what is done.
- There is a mish-mash of approaches to implementing customer success management—different definitions, goals, issues, processes, and metrics.
- As validated by the research participants, delivering both customer success and the customer experiences that help drive customer success is everyone's business, but the message, the motivation, and the money all start at the top.
- Only a small percentage of organizations in the study noted that a senior manager was in charge of customer success management.
- Some participants questioned the "internal commitment" of the leadership team in regard to customer success management.
- There were surprisingly few differences between how more mature organizations and less mature organizations responded to the implementation of customer success management, however, the more mature organizations had a greater number of metrics in place to measure results.
- Some concerns were voiced regarding if the appropriate structure was in place.
- Many on-premise organizations attempting to implement customer success appear to be unprepared for the transition (inadequate resources, undetermined structure, ill-defined processes). In some cases, they are especially unprepared for the required change in culture, and hence, face a real possibility of failure.

Leadership Recommendations

- Take a holistic approach. Customer success implementation requires a systemic approach firmly embedded in the culture

and directly linked to the organization blueprint—this is a leadership requirement.[5]
- Clearly formulate and then articulate the organization blueprint over and over again with the emphasis on customer success.
- Take the time to formulate and communicate the lifetime value of key customers. The size of this number has wonderful motivational impact on both supplier leadership and supplier employees.
- Get your "physical." Start with an assessment or a readiness review, if you are in the early stages of customer success, or a health check, if you desire moving to the next level of performance. The elasticity of your culture assessment and the depth of your blueprint are key indicators of your achievement potential.
- Measure the metrics that matter most: brand quality, win rate, retention, growth, customer and employee loyalty, customer experience, and time to value.
- Get the big dogs off the porch...if your executives don't get it, the pack doesn't hunt.
- Link executive compensation to customer success management performance.
- Let your stars shine. Publicly recognize employee actions that deliver on the customer success promise (especially in the early days).
- The ability to scale is a big deal. Start customer success efforts with key accounts to clearly define and refine all aspects of the supplier-customer success process, and learn as you go. Deliver adequate high touch where needed (one-to-one), gradually find ways to enhance efficiency touching one-to-few, and build the capabilities to touch one-to-many.
- Get the big bills out of your wallet. Invest as if your future is at stake (it is).
- Reality for pure cloud organizations: Unless your offering is

lightyears beyond your galaxy of competitors, you have no choice but to embrace a culture and a blueprint of customer success.
- Reality for traditional organizations: Transforming to a culture of customer success won't work in many organizations—remember those 30% customer-oblivious organizations? Like asking a bluegrass band to play only heavy metal, the desired transformation is just too extreme. Conduct a readiness review to determine if the probability deserves the investment in time and pain. If so, aggressively invest and implement change management following a proven change management model.

Leading Brilliant Change

Do you dread leading, managing, or directing the change to customer success? You may have heard that:
1. Important change takes three to five years, or more.
2. Change is really hard.
3. People may revolt, and some will quit.
4. Chaos may ensue.
5. People really, really hate change.

Yes, important change is not easy—it will take some time, and some people may not like it. However, the oft-spoke truism that people hate change is flat wrong.

Think about it: If that were true, people around the world would own automobiles like those driven in Havana today! Driving a 1957 Chevy would be the norm, because if people dreaded change, they'd keep the car they have and just fix it when it breaks. How about flat-screen televisions? Millions of people are buying (changing) televisions when they have perfectly good ones at home. Where is all this resistance to change we hear about? Finally, think about a time when you were offered a big promotion. Did you turn it down because it meant that you would have to make all kinds of changes, such as requisitioning new furniture to fit your larger office, ordering new business cards to reflect your new importance, and adjusting your spending habits to accommodate a new, heftier paycheck?

True, these personal examples are a bit tongue in cheek, yet the fundamental tenets of personal change are the same—people don't resist change per se, they are "change neutral." In fact, they readily embrace what they view as "good" change, but they resist (sometimes quite tenaciously) what they see as "bad" change.

Figure 6.2, the Personal Change Meter, looks at four of the key dimensions people consider (consciously or unconsciously) when evaluating change that impacts their level of support or resistance. Adding up the scores gives a rough indicator of change "goodness."

Figure 6.2 Personal Change Meter

RESISTENCE				CHANGE DIMENSION				SUPPORT	
Faulty Training				Rationality				Makes Clear Sense	
-5	-4	-3	-2	-1	0	+1	+2	+3	+4	+5
No Trust				Commitment				Believe	
-5	-4	-3	-2	-1	0	+1	+2	+3	+4	+5
Penalties				Fairness				Balanced	
-5	-4	-3	-2	-1	0	+1	+2	+3	+4	+5
Pain				Value				Gain	
-5	-4	-3	-2	-1	0	+1	+2	+3	+4	+5
BAD CHANGE								**GOOD CHANGE**	

Below are examples of the range of mindset in each of the four dimensions, along with tips on how to turn the bad into good.

Rationality: Does It Make Sense?

Good Change: "Yes, the world is flat, our market is changing, we need to do something, and these new initiatives make clear sense. I get it." Or...

Bad Change: "Cripes sakes, who thought this one up? Why in the world would we do this now? Is this just a ploy to set us up to be sold and make the executives rich?"

Quick Tips to Move the Meter to the Right: Make sure that you have a logic path supported by facts and figures to make your case. Provide industry examples to build credibility. Get the word out.

Commitment: Will Management Follow Through?

Good Change: "I believe that our management team is truly committed and will do everything possible to make us successful, even when times are tough." Or...

Bad Change: "Yeah, I've heard this before. Just wait. If sales dip for 90 days I bet this becomes just another program-of-the-month, and we are back to business as usual."

Quick Tips to Move the Meter to the Right: If you and your management have a good record of following through, then make reference to those times. If not, build and communicate a detailed plan that demonstrates that the changes are well thought out, resources are being allocated, and success measures are being put in place. Look and publicize wins, and communicate zero tolerance for those not playing by the new rules. For example, everyone will take notice of what happens to the top seller who lands a big account but sells the customer an inappropriate solution. Does he still make the President's Club, or is he put on probation? Appropriate actions shout commitment.

Fairness: Is It Fair to the Customer, My Peers, and Me?

Good Change: "It appears balanced and reasonable to all key stakeholders." Or...

Bad Change: "Boy, it looks as though X and Y are really getting a bad deal in this. They are really paying a big price compared to everyone else."

Quick Tips to Move the Meter to the Right: Do an impact analysis of all those affected, and then think about how you can make adjustments that people will see as being more reasonable. Fairness counts.

Value: How Good a Deal Is It for Me?

Good Change: "Wow! What a personal opportunity to broaden my skills, become more marketable, and make more money." Or...

Bad Change: "This is scary. I don't know if I can do what they are talking about. I don't think I'll like it. This could be a real hassle. This looks like a lot of work."

Quick Tips to Move the Meter to the Right: The first three factors are important, but they shrink in comparison to this last factor. Remember that people use facts to justify doing things they want to do. Recognize that people will work for gain but fight to retain, so make sure you start by telling people what will stay the same before telling them what will change. Work really hard to demonstrate how people will benefit from what is new, but try not to take away something of value. If you want people to change behavior, remember that this is a selling job—point out the what, the why, and the benefits. And be prepared to communicate it again and again.

Leading change does not have to be a painful ordeal. Use the Personal Change Meter to help make all change good change.

Remember, brilliant customer success is not for woosies.

Conclusion

If done correctly, customer success offers the promise of great rewards. For many organizations the transition to customer success management is a requirement for survival. Although there are potholes on the path, the trail is well marked, and the summit is achievable. So get off your lounge chair and take the dive off the high board into the brisk waters of customer success.

Good luck on your journey.

References and Notes

Introduction

1. Alexander, James A., EdD. 2016. *Customer Success: Managing the Customer Experience for Loyalty and Profit.* Alexander Consulting and Service Strategies Corporation. (A big tip of the hat to my colleague and friend, Ben Stephens, who was my co-collaborator in conducting the research.)
2. Ibid.
3. "An Executive Primer to Customer Success Management." April 2014. Thought Leadership Paper. Forrester.
4. Mehta. Nick, Dan Steinman, and Lincoln Murphy. 2016. *Customer Success: How Innovative Companies Are Reducing Churn and Growing Recurring Revenue.* Hoboken, NJ: John Wiley & Sons, Inc.

Overview

1. Mehta, Nick. October 18, 2015. "The 5 Kinds of Customer Success." Gainsight, Venturebeat.
2. Drucker, Peter F. 1974. *Management: Tasks, Responsibilities, Practices*. New York: Harper & Row.

Chapter 1

1. Albrecht, Karl and Ron Zemke. 1985. *Service America in the New Economy*. Dow Jones-Irwin. McGraw Hill Companies.
2. Robinson, Floren and Justin M. Brown. March 2012. "How to Make Your Company Think Like a Customer." Accenture Customer Relationship Management white paper.

Chapter 2

1. Alexander, James A., EdD. January 26, 2015. "Brilliant CX: The 7 Things Your Customers Want, Expect, and Deserve." LinkedIn Blog.
2. Goodman, John. 2014. *Customer Experience 3.0: High-Profit Strategies in the Age of Techno Service*. New York: AMACOM.
3. Ibid.
4. Ibid.
5. Alexander, James A., EdD. December 10, 2015. "Brilliant CX: Compressing the Cycle Time of Trust." LinkedIn Blog.
6. Alexander, James A., EdD. January 27, 2016. "Brilliant CX Tool: Harnessing Hassel." LinkedIn Blog.

Chapter 4

1. Check out Natero's "Customer Success Performance Metrics" (October 15, 2015) for a good primer. www.natero.com.

2. "Predictive Analytics for Customer Success." Natero Blog. http://learn.natero.com/predictive-analytics-for-customer-success.
3. Szundi, George. January 27, 2016. "Designing Effective Customer Health Scores." Natero Blog. http://blog.natero.com/designing-effective-customer-health-score.
4. "What's Missing in Your Customer Success Program?" August 20, 2015. Virent Webcast for TSIA.

Chapter 5

1. Alexander, James A., EdD. November 4, 2015. "Brilliant CX: Send Champagne with the Roses." LinkedIn Blog.

Chapter 6

1. Schein, E.J. 1992. *Organizational Culture and Leadership*. 2nd edition. San Francisco: Jossey-Bass.
2. Kotter, J.P. and J.L. Heskett. 1992. *Corporate Culture and Performance*. New York: Free Press.
3. Alexander, J.A. 1999. "A Test of a Rapid Developer Model." In K.P. Kuchinke (ed.). Conference proceedings. Academy of Human Resource Development.
4. The core principals of strategic account management and customer success are the same — tailored to the account, emphasis on personal relationships, hard and soft data, with ongoing analysis, meeting the individual needs of key customer personnel, and so on. Think of CSM as SAM on steroids, deeper wider analytics, more focus on details, and everything done faster.
5. Steinman, Dan. "The Ten Laws of Customer Success." Gainsight. http://www.gainsight.com/resource/the-10-laws-of-customer-success/.

About the Author

James "Alex" Alexander, EdD, researches, publishes, advises, trains, and speaks on transforming organizations into brilliant customer success businesses that create loyal customers, drive profitable sales, and dominate the competition. Contact Alex at alex@alexanderstrategists.com.

Acknowledgements

A special hats off to Ben Stephens, my friend and longtime colleague, who I collaborated with to design and implement the customer success research that was a core component of the book. Also a big thanks to Service Strategies Corporation for all their support.

    Much appreciation to my buddy of several decades, Jamey Renwick, for her fast eagle-eye feedback on the text.

    And a bucketload of gratitude to Suzanne for her brilliant support on this book and on all things I do.